RE-MEMBERING FRANKENSTEIN

Healing the monster in every man

G. H. Ellis MD

authorHOUSE®

AuthorHouse™
1663 Liberty Drive
Bloomington, IN 47403
www.authorhouse.com
Phone: 1-800-839-8640

First published by AuthorHouse 7/26/2011

ISBN: 978-1-4634-0066-8 (sc)
ISBN: 978-1-4634-0065-1 (e)

Library of Congress Control Number: 2011908331

Printed in the United States of America

Any people depicted in stock imagery provided by Thinkstock are models, and such images are being used for illustrative purposes only. Certain stock imagery © Thinkstock.

This book is printed on acid-free paper.

ACKNOWLEDGEMENTS

I began this project seven years ago and its completion is a credit to many assistants. I am grateful for much needed inspiration, wisdom, and encouragement. The inspiration ultimately belongs to Mary Shelley for her gift of *Frankenstein*. My youngest daughter purchased a copy for a high school English class, and I read it because it was in the house. I immediately connected the monster story to my psychological journey. Additional inspiration came from movie artists that provided images that resonated with my inner monster.

The wisdom that I try to pass along is that of C.G. Jung and his followers, especially Edward Edinger, Robert Moore, Robert Johnson, Robert Bly, and other quoted authors. I am especially indebted to Robert Moore for his personal assistance in healing my inner monster.

For review and comments I am indebted to Mike and KC Anderson, Rick Smith, Rik Spier, Jim Eggers, and especially Janice Mutch, my "good witch" friend. She spent hours with me clarifying my thinking and providing encouragement.

I bear sole responsibility for the contents of this book and all remaining errors of content, confusion, spelling, grammar, and syntax. I assure the readers that the hundreds of hours my wonderful wife, Janet S. Ellis, spent in editing and decoding my writing style has made the book less tedious for them. No words could adequately express my appreciation for her efforts.

PREFACE

Frankenstein is the story of Victor Frankenstein who suffers the consequences of creating a humanoid monster. *Re-Membering Frankenstein* is a hypothetical exercise of imagining that Victor is an acquaintance struggling with life issues. The reader is invited to imagine being his analyst or friend who listens to his story and hears how Victor reacts to the common psychological issues that confront men, particularly near mid-life. Mary Shelley's story is man's monster struggle. In Victor's case there are two monsters: the one he creates in the laboratory and the other is the psychological internal monster that is present in every man. The main characters and events represent relevant metaphors for the psychological struggles of men.

This book is intended as a tool to assist men who are transitioning in life. The concepts, exercises, and questions of the book are intended to accelerate a man's therapeutic progress. The book may also be useful to women seeking to understand more about male psychology. I have no goal more grandiose than hoping the reader concludes that the several hours spent with this book have been at least as valuable as an hour of therapy, and much less expensive.

Frankenstein captivated its contemporary audience immediately upon publication in 1818. Two centuries later the Frankenstein image is a universal anthropomorphic symbol of hideous terror and gigantic power. Author Mary Shelley contacted a deep mythic presence of destructive power present in the human psyche, an entity that exists in each of us. This entity is "the monster," a living part of our shadow capable of vengeance and injury.

Frankenstein belongs to the literary genre of the epic battle between the forces of good and evil. Fictional monsters such as Dracula, the Cyclops, Hannibal Lector, Wolfman, King Kong, the Wicked Witch, and Satan captivate us because they express a part of our human shadow. Secretly our own shadow monster pulls for these villains. Other mythic monsters such as dragons, snakes, or Godzilla represent our dangerous animalistic instincts. Malevolent kings and tyrants such as Caesar or Darth Vader represent our capacity to oppress others. We are drawn to these psychological metaphors because they induce a flow of libido from the good and evil potentials within us. The special appeal of the Frankenstein monster is its secret and personal identity like our personal monster.

While primarily concerned with one's personal monster, at times monsters in the collective psyche are also mentioned. Personal monsters can be agents of much collective injury. Murderous Columbine teens, greed-driven CEO's, and drug traffickers are obvious examples. Genocide perpetrators like Hitler, Pol Pot or Stalin are the worst examples.

Bad News—Good News

The bad news is that the forces that isolate and activate monster potentials are powerful. Genetic and cultural inhibitions create resistance to monster work. We (men) need encouragement to undergo therapeutic reflection of our monsters, not only because they have the capacity to create suffering, but our monsters also carry much personal libido, which if not accessed will spawn depression, isolation, and loss of joy.

The really bad news is that monster work is scary, difficult, complex, and confusing. To acknowledge our shadows is terrifying. To realize that our evil capacity will never leave us requires courage over despair. Simply put: monster work is sisyphusian, like rolling rocks uphill in the dark.

The good news is that most of us already have enough relationship with the inner monster to restrain it from murderous atrocities. Serial killers are impossible to rehabilitate, but the average Joe can integrate his monster adequately to significantly enhance his happiness, and that alone makes the effort worthwhile.

The better news is that we have an inner source of courage, the universal desire to become fully authentic. This drive toward reinvigoration helps overcome the fear of confronting the monster. The best news is that doing our monster work will expand our kindness; enhance our sense of completeness; and provide a new source of joy.

Before we join Victor Frankenstein on his monster adventure, some background information is useful about the following:

1. The character metaphors

2. Terms and concepts from Jungian psychology which are the orientation and bias of this book

3. Pertinent aspects of Mary Shelley's life

4. The myth of Prometheus

1. METAPHORS

THE METPHOR of RE-MEMBERING

The book's title, *Re-Membering Frankenstein*, is a pun with multiple meanings. The first is to sustain the story of *Frankenstein* in active memory, to remember it not only for its exquisite prose, but as a literary classic treasure for its characters who serve as the images of a man's totality.

The second meaning of the title involves the definition of a member as a body part, especially an arm or a leg. Victor Frankenstein sews together body parts to assemble his monster. The psychological metaphor is that split-off parts of the psyche get reassembled into an inner psychic monster. Disconnecting a portion of our libido from our core being, our psychological Self, is like cutting away an arm or leg. Once completed the inner monster has destructive potential. Achieving psychic balance requires re-attaching (re-membering) the cut-off parts (members) into consciousness.

A third nuance of the "re-membering" pun is that of returning a person (member) back into a group. Every person has a cast of inner characters and personalities that comprise the totality of his psyche. Victor abandons his monster. He also neglects others in his outer life who are metaphors for cast-out inner-life personalities. Re-membering would require Victor's ego to re-accept those exiled shadow personality characters back into the cast of his life's play.

The fourth aspect of the title's pun is to remember what happened to Victor Frankenstein as a warning to heed the tragedy awaiting those who repeat his errors. *Frankenstein* is a horror story because the monster perpetrates murder; it is a tragedy because Victor fails to avert the murders despite repeated confrontations with his monster and opportunities to change.

MONSTER METAPHORS

There are two monsters in Mary Shelley's novel. The literal one is the creature that Victor Frankenstein creates in his laboratory, a visible monstrosity composed of cut-off organs and limbs from dead persons. The second monster is the monster that lives within the psyche of Victor Frankenstein, an invisible source of potential destruction.

Multiple descriptions apply to monsters. One physical definition is a hideous creature. Victor Frankenstein's monster exceeds eight feet in height and has yellow eyes with grotesque facial features. People shudder and run when they see his ugly face and frightening stature. A person's shadow is also hideous and society demands it be hidden.

Sometimes a monster refers to something huge or powerful. We call large people or things, monstrous. The largest hamburger at Hardee's restaurant is the monster burger. The shadow can be overwhelmingly powerful.

Monster has a specific medical definition of a grotesquely deformed infant, especially one with abnormal parts or limbs. Victor is the creator and father of a being he immediately abandons and rejects because of its grotesqueness.

Some beings are monsters due to injuries with scars. The iconic cinema image of the Frankenstein monster is the "bolt-through-the-neck" headshot. Scars are typical features of horror film characters. Psychological scars are suffering associated with shameful childhood experiences. Thus the Frankenstein monster is a metaphor for the scarring that creates a psychological monster.

A fourth definition of monster refers to a person who is cruel and wicked and performs evil acts. The evil perpetrated by Frankenstein's monster is murder. Thus Shelley's fictional creation is giant, hideous, deformed, and evil: a monster by all accounts.

VICTOR FRANKENSTEIN'S METAPHOR

Frank means honest. Stein is a mug, a vessel for a fluid, usually beer or alcohol spirits. Thus Frankenstein connotes an honest man holding spirits within.

Victor means one who conquers. Thus Victor Frankenstein is a man who fights for victory. The battle is with his creature. The essence of the combat is Victor's desire to control his monster's spirit. We shall see that Victor pays a heavy price for this victory.

The narrative of *Frankenstein* provides clues to inner monster formation. Victor's intellectual interests, hubris, and devotion to his father and mother create his inner monster. Pressures from his extended family and society also contribute. The development of Victor's inner monster parallels Victor's creation of the laboratory monster. The drama hinges on whether Victor can heal the outer and inner monsters.

2. THE JUNGIAN PERSPECTIVE

JUNGIAN STRUCTURE

Depth psychology [synonyms are Jungian analysis and analytical psychology] is this book's psychological basis and bias. It is grounded in the tenet that each individual has a unique psychic life to discover and live. The goal of depth psychology is individuation, the achievement of an integrated psychic totality. The central psychic construct of depth psychology is the existence of a center of totality, the "Self", that contains one's personal agenda for individuation.

An archetype is an organizational structure for behaviors that is instinctually human and not personal. The term archetype comes from Carl Jung, the Swiss psychologist. He believed that the human brain evolved specific patterns of responding to emotional content. Jung discovered archetypes through cross-cultural empirical studies. "Arche" means ancient as in archeology and implies an inherited legacy of thousands of years. For utility an archetype is given the name of a mythic character whose personality describes the cluster of behaviors and responses we associate with the archetype. For example, the personalities of the ancient gods, Ares and Aphrodite, the Greek gods of war and passion, are archetypal images of how humans make love and war.

In the Jungian lexicon the psyche is the aggregate organization of the feelings, thoughts, and motives that consciously or unconsciously influence a person. The totality of one's psyche is the Self (the "S" is capitalized). It is an archetype of wholeness and unification of a person.

The psyche includes the ego archetype, which is one's conscious awareness. Our ego thinks and devises our conscious intentions; however, it is only a portion of our totality. The ego is a necessary structure for cohesion and to bridge the inner world with the outer.

The shadow archetype refers to a reservoir of repressed and denied traits that become organized within the unconscious of a person. Desires that society or the individual cannot or will not acknowledge or allow are relegated to a part of the psyche called the shadow. The shadow is an integral part of the Self, but it is experienced outside the ego. The monster is the agent of the destructive potential of the shadow archetype.

The struggle for relationship between a man and his monster is an encounter with the archetype of the soul. The soul is the outward flow and expression of the totality of the Self. The soul has a quality of uniqueness and is the core essence of a person. One is described as having lost his soul when an observer believes a person no longer expresses his authentic nature.

External forces that modulate our soul through contact with

the Self are spirit. Spirit has a divine external quality of an outer purpose in contrast to soul, which is intrinsic. We talk of holiday spirit, spirits of the dead, and nature spirits like the wind. Team spirit is a connection and will to support one's team. Spirit is experienced as originating from an outer source to move us emotionally. Divine spirit is felt as a connection to humanity and the universe. It is god-like because it influences our internal god-image, the Self.

Dreams are a mainstay of all schools of psychotherapy, but particularly psychoanalysis and Jungian depth psychology. Men's dreams are presented to demonstrate common motifs in a man's therapy.

Complexes are theme-clustered behaviors such as the mother-complex and father-complex.

Dialogues with inner characters are named active imagination. The analysand is active (consciously awake) and engages a character in conversation to elicit and clarify its needs in the psyche. Examples of active imagination are included in this book to support the discussion and to encourage the analysand to discover its usefulness.

Other important archetypes expressed in *Frankenstein* include the divine child, inferior function, the anima, and feminine justice.

3. MARY SHELLEY

LIFE OF THE AUTHOR

Mary Shelley was born Mary Wollstonecraft in England in 1797. Her academic parents were Enlightenment Age progressives and political activists. Her father, William Godwin, was a Calvinist preacher who turned to atheism and became a teacher. He was a mediocre author by his own admission, but loved writers, marrying one, Mary Shelly's mother, the first Mary Wollstonecraft.

Mary Shelley's mother was a free spirit who left an abusive father and traveled to London to become an accomplished feminist writer. Mary Shelley's principled mother kept her maiden name, a forceful statement of independence in the pre-Victorian days at the end of the eighteenth century. Mary Shelley's father supported his wife's feminist agenda. In 1794 she bore Fanny, Mary's illegitimate older sister, three years prior to Mary's birth; Fanny's father abandoned them.

William Godwin and Shelley's mother had a libertine attitude toward sex and a suspicious contempt for the institution of marriage; however, they acquiesced to society and married five months before Mary was born. Tragically Mary Shelley's mother died of puerperal sepsis from retained placental fragments eleven days after the birth of Mary; her father named her Mary Wollstonecraft in remembrance of her mother. Her father remarried when Mary was four. His new wife was a stereotypical wicked stepmother.

William Godwin idealized and kept company with many talented London writers. He adored a young poet named Percy Bysshe Shelley. Mary's father often invited him over to the house. Percy Shelley found Mary intellectually stimulating and easily distracted him from the boredom of his stultifying wife and child. They escaped together: Mary (age seventeen) freed herself from the stepmother and childhood she detested; Percy (age nineteen) abandoned his London family responsibilities. Mary Wollstonecraft and Percy Shelley joined several other free-spirited writers to tour Europe. They traveled and co-habited for several years with Mary experiencing two pregnancies before they married.

This traveling group of writers "summered" each year in Switzerland or Italy. History has proven the enormous talent and genius of this group that included John Keats, Lord Byron, Percy Bysshe Shelley, John Polodori, and Mary Shelley. This communal group of young adults also included Mary's stepsister, Claire, whose contempt for her own mother (Mary's stepmother) corroborated Mary's painful experience. Claire had her lustful eyes focused on Lord Byron. Although Byron was a known lecher, Claire was the seducer in this relationship. During 1816 Claire insisted they summer in Geneva, Switzerland so that Claire would be near her heartthrob, Lord Byron. Like a sixties college commune, they wrote, played, and made love out of sight of disapproving English busybodies. Percy reportedly invited participation in communal sexual fantasies. (Wolfe)

Percy was a rising star-poet of the London literary circles. Like his compatriots, John Keats and Lord Byron, their talents and lifestyles were exceedingly fast-tracked resulting in literary immortality, but had short lives tainted with immorality. These writers shared stories and critiqued one another's writings with intense scrutiny and prolonged conscious deliberation. The character names of *Frankenstein* convey intentional metaphors, a result of the group's heated debates.

While Mary Wollstonecraft and Percy Shelley were consorting in Switzerland, he was still inconveniently married to pregnant Harriet Westbrook. Poets will be poets, but one is hard-pressed to dismiss Percy's appalling lack of responsibility as a husband and father. Harriet, alone in London, delivered a son in November 1814.

Meanwhile, seventeen-year-old Mary Wollstonecraft was simultaneously pregnant with his baby and gave birth to a boy prematurely in February 1815. The child died within a week. Shortly she became pregnant again and eleven months later baby William was born to Mary and Percy in January 1816.

For Mary Shelley these were seminal years (pun intended), particularly the fall of 1816, when at the Swiss mountain villa after reading German ghost stories, Lord Byron, suggested a contest in which the writers each devised their own horror story to share. This was Mary's inspiration for *Frankenstein*. History proves she won the contest. She refined the manuscript and it was published two years later.

A side note to the horror story contest is that John Polodori, Byron's friend and personal physician, wrote a dismal tale of a skull-head peeping Tom. Later he became famous with the success of a vampire poem about a womanizing nobleman in London entitled *Ruthvein* (red vein). *Ruthvein* was the basis of Bram Stoker's original vampire character, Dracula. Polodori knew the cad well: his vampire was a poorly disguised Byron whose seductions of women embarrassed even the least moral of his friends. For example, Byron impregnated Mary's stepsister, Claire, and dispassionately abandoned her. Byron was the author of the epic poem, *Don Juan*, an unconscious braggadocio of his sexual proclivity.

While finishing *Frankenstein,* significant events happened in Mary's life. Harriet, Percy's wife, unable to recover from a combination of post-partum depression, heartbreak, and general aristocratic humiliation, committed suicide late in 1816. Percy was minimally aggrieved. I speculate that Mary Shelley had a complex emotional response to marrying Percy. Her joy was likely tempered knowing that his libertine sexual mores contributed to the death of Harriet. In *Frankenstein,* the moral lapse of Victor's face-saving silence causes the death of an innocent female character, Justine. Three weeks after Harriet's suicide, Percy benevolently married Mary Wollstonecraft and legitimized their son.

While Mary was finishing *Frankenstein,* Percy was working on one of his epic poems, the four-volume opus, *Prometheus Unbound.* Published in 1820, *Prometheus Unbound* is a sequel to Aeschylus' play, *Prometheus Bound,* concerning the rehabilitation and freeing of Prometheus. The play implies that technological advancements require a conscious and renewed reverence of nature and God.

Percy felt the nineteenth century was recreating the myth of Prometheus. He feared that the hubris of technology and industry would bring evil. Arguably the advent of high-tech wars and nuclear bombs proves that Percy was accurately prescient. In Percy Shelley's opus, Prometheus is set free signaling Percy's belief that knowledge, although inevitable and dangerous, could with conscious diligence, ultimately bring goodness.

Mary and Percy were bonded into a dyad, an archetypal twinning wherein each person expresses portions of the other's psyche. Percy's obsessing and pillow talk reviling the public's worship of science likely influenced Mary to incorporate the Prometheus myth into *Frankenstein* as the obsessive character of Victor Frankenstein, and subtitle the story, *"The Modern Prometheus."*

Mary Shelley was living closely enough with Percy and Byron to observe their personal monsters. Percy loved sailing and named his boat "The Don Juan," in honor of his friend, Lord Byron. Don Juan well suited the play toy for the shameless and reckless side of Percy. We cannot be sure that that Percy used his boat for romantic trysts, but he was interested in group sex and was unfaithful to his first wife from the beginning. When Mary gave birth to their premature infant in 1815, she was ill and desperately trying to keep her baby alive while Percy was off hunting, a recurrence of his husbandly neglect. Mary's older half-sister committed suicide, arguably from feeling unloved by her inadequate stepfather, abused by her evil mother, and depressed after Lord Byron rejected her.

Tragically, Percy (age 30) died at sea when the Don Juan capsized. Mary Shelley continued writing novels to support her family. She suffered the personal, social, and economic pains of widowhood and being a single parent. Her good friends Keats and Byron died young: Keats at age 26 probably from tuberculosis; Byron at age 36 of a war injury suffered during a mercenary military adventure. Death thus became a recurrent theme in Mary's writings that mirrored her life. The post-partum death of mother and peri-natal death of her son are reflected in *Frankenstein*. Mary wrote in her journal about a dream of rubbing the life back into her dead baby; her fantasy of restoring life to her mother became Victor Frankenstein's passion.

The back-story of Mary Shelley's novel is more than juicy gossip. It links the fiction of *Frankenstein* to the suffering that is caused by good people with creative brilliance that are unconscious of their monstrous capacities. Unreflectively discharging his libido, Percy caused enormous suffering to his family; similarly Victor Frankenstein caused deaths from unreflectively and irresponsibly discharging his creative capacities in his laboratory.

THE PROMETHEUS MYTH

Shelley's 1818 literary audience was familiar with classical Greek mythologies such as Prometheus. Being less true today, a review of the myth will help us understand Shelley's analogy of *Frankenstein* to Prometheus. The subtitle of the novel, *or the Modern Prometheus*, expresses Mary Shelley's belief that Victor Frankenstein's struggle with his monster represents a problem of modernity, i.e., new science was bringing unforeseen maladies.

Iapetus, the father of Prometheus, was in good favor with Zeus. He had helped Zeus overthrow his father, Cronus, to become the next king of the gods. As a reward Zeus allowed Iapetus and his sons, Prometheus and Epimetheus, to interact freely with humans. Prometheus is a name that means forethought: pro (fore) and metheus (thought). He was a devisor of ideas, the patron god of technology. Prometheus's brother is named Epimetheus, meaning afterthought. He is the experience of realizing too late the consequences of actions.

Prometheus had compassion for humans and decided to give them fire. OOPS! Although well-intentioned, Prometheus's gift caused unforeseen catastrophe to humans. Talking and playing with humans is one thing, but giving them fire was heresy to Zeus. Enraged, Zeus sentenced Prometheus to be eternally chained to a rock. Every day an eagle would swoop down upon the chained-up Prometheus and eat a hole into his liver. At night the liver regenerated and the cycle was replayed every day, a cycle of eternal suffering. Recurrent suffering is a metaphor for unconsciously repeating mistakes without necessary reflection to grow beyond the suffering. In Percy Shelley's *Prometheus Unbound,* Prometheus eventually is released from the cycle of suffering, analogous to the process of achieving consciousness.

Zeus was not finished with his vengeance upon Prometheus and his human friends. Zeus had his blacksmith, Hephaestus, make a box container and filled it with godly powers that caused havoc because they were too powerful for humans to control. Zeus was in effect ranting, "You want to play with fire (godly powers)? OK, well I'll give you something to play with, a box of supernatural marbles!"

This box was given to Epimetheus's wife, Pandora. Her name means Pan (all) and Dora (gifts of the gods). The gifts of the gods are powers that prove to be dangerous, like atomic power. The result is pan-human pain and suffering. Poor Pandora, she just wanted a quick peek. Too late! All the ill effects from the divine gifts immediately escaped unbounded to torture mankind. Like Eve, a woman who defied the patriarchal authority, Pandora was blamed for all the troubles of humanity. Only hope remained in the box, i.e., of the gods' gifts, hope is the only one controlled by humans.

Epimetheus, the god of afterthought, was no help. He is literally the god of "oops, shit happened!" Today his counterpart is a drug company that sells new drugs only to discover lethal side effects after the marketing blitz. It is also the engineer who makes a super-highway and then discovers traffic congestion and air pollution.

Victor Frankenstein wishes to give humanity the technology of resurrection. Creativity is a divine attribute represented by Prometheus' gift of fire. Just as Prometheus did not foresee the consequences of handing fire over to the humans, Victor has no clear view of the consequences of creating his monster. He constructed the monster from the dead and then immediately abandoned him out of horror and fear. Victor lacked any planning for dealing with the actions of his creature. He released the contents of his Pandora's Box that became a string of deaths across Europe. His only remaining possession was expressed as an afterthought: the hope that the sea adventurer, Robert Walton, could learn from his tragedy.

The Prometheus myth implies that the cosmos is structured such that creativity is divine inspiration, but living with the results is a human experience. New information and technology is inevitable, and so are unforeseen consequences. Hope is the gift that helps humans deal with the unforeseen consequences.

Re-Membering Frankenstein expresses the parallel psychological metaphor: Creating a monster within the psyche is a normal human experience. Creation is a divine gift, but the human must work out how to deal with it. Hope gives us courage to move forward to assist our ego to deal with our inner monster.

FINAL INTRODUCTORY NOTES

Shelley's original text has no name for the created monster, referring to it only as the creature, daemon, or monster. The absence of a name makes it surreal: a dream-like, amorphous, and unknowable character that frightens us.

Two versions of *Frankenstein* have been published: the original in 1818 and Shelley's revision in 1831. As there are numerous publication sources for this classic so the selected quotes are referenced by chapter and paragraph from the 1831 version.

LETTER ONE

The Prometheus myth ends with the hope that remains in Pandora's Box; *Frankenstein* begins and ends with the hope Victor Frankenstein's tale will save the soul of Robert Walton, a ship captain who rescues Victor from an Arctic iceberg. The prologue consists of letters written by Robert Walton to his sister. The central novel details the story of Victor Frankenstein and his monster, and the novel concludes in chapter twenty-four, an epilogue that returns to Robert's homebound letters.

Robert Walton's first letter explains to his sister, Margaret, that he is in Baltic Russia impatiently awaiting the spring thaw to embark on an exploration to discover a northwest passage to the Pacific through the Arctic Ocean. His stated purpose is to advance commercial shipping access to the Orient; but his true agenda is to garner fame from discovering a passage that has been the failed quest of many previous sea captains.

His name, Bob, the sea adventurer, implies bobbing up and down on the sea. Bob has no awareness of what lies below the surface of the ocean, a metaphor for being unaware of his unconscious. His last name is Walton. This is a pun, a "wall-of-ton", a heavy burden or an impassible obstruction. His first burden is the arctic winter and ice jams that are delaying his departure. He also carries an unconscious load, his inner grandiosity.

Walton is unaware (at sea) that his longing for the sea adventure is his soul requesting his inner exploration. Robert represents the young man who can either mature into wholeness or die in isolation. He is at sea in the adventure of life, conscious of neither the depth of the experience nor the dangers of the journey.

In psychotherapeutic terms the time has arrived to launch the journey to discover the Self. The drive to adventure is a thrust of libido from an unconscious source to bring unlived potentials into awareness. Accomplishing a conscious connection with the soul will make one feel alive. The inner hand of the Self begins the personal adventure by knocking on the ego's door to invite the ego to partner with aspects of the psyche unknown to it. Invitation is too weak a word; like a request from Don Corleone, it is an offer the ego cannot refuse.

There is a feminine aspect of this call to adventure. It has a flowing and wavy quality. Walton is a typical man who charges ahead like a bull. He denies the feminine part of his soul and seeks a woman to carry that sensitivity. Robert Walton's feminine sensitivity resides in Margaret Saville, his sister. Her name, Saville, connotes the power to "save the ill one." A recurring theme in men's psychology is the importance of feminine energy to heal a man. Feminine energy refers to both help from outer women and the emotional resources of our souls.

Walton's first letter announces the initiation of his journey. His ego has no clue he has been called from his soul to move toward wholeness. Robert simply has great energy to go exploring. Consider this dream of a man age thirty-five beginning therapy for "mid-life confusion:"

The dreamer is standing on a roller coaster track wearing snow skis. He tries to purchase new skis but cannot find two that match. He is among pleasant friends. Next the ski track changes to a three-dimensional labyrinth of impossible complexity. The track is composed of black discs that are puzzle pieces. To solve the puzzle the dreamer manipulates the discs, but as he attempts to fit the pieces together, they change shapes and fly larvae begin to grow upon them. The complexity of the puzzle leaves the dreamer exhausted. He gives up in confusion and runs away.

This dream says an inner adventure has begun along a difficult track that the dreamer currently does not understand, aptly describing the psychotherapeutic landscape ahead for this man. He will experience a cold place where skis are needed to navigate the terrain. It will be a roller coaster ride along a slippery slope where it is easy to lose footing and control. The dreamer doesn't have the right equipment and the right skis cannot simply be purchased or invented by the ego. The complexity of the three-dimensional labyrinth is a foreshadowing of the depth of the journey that will require thinking in multiple dimensions, i.e., functions of his personality that are not currently engaged. The ego will have to relinquish control because the puzzling nature of the adventure will require more than the ego's ability to figure things out. He will have to deal with the black discs. Black is the color of the shadow. The fly larvae are annoying, primitive creatures that are creepy and disgusting. But insect larvae also pupate into flying (fully alive) creatures. The challenge to the dreamer is to accept and transcend the ugliness of his fly larvae as he deciphers the puzzle of the way (the Tao to the Buddhist). He also must resist the temptation to give up.

Victor Frankenstein could have brought this dream to his initial therapy session for it accurately predicts his future. Initial dreams have value for the therapist in prognosticating and guiding the progress of the analysand. Optimistically there are unknown but helpful friends in the background. One aspect warranting emphasis is the universal requirement to deal with shadow contents. This man's therapist predicted that he would become confused, lonely, and resistant. He would try hard to "figure it out himself," but his frustrated ego would need assistance. When close to making transformative changes he would feel like bugs and larvae were crawling on him. He would contemplate running away from therapy. The complexity of the puzzle pieces suggests that the analysand has a great deal of work ahead.

Like the dreamer of the ski track puzzle above, Robert Walton too is just beginning his journey/personal transition. He doesn't know it yet, but he has embarked on a psychic adventure to confront his shadow. His ego believes he is actively constructing an outer adventure to discover a northwest passage, but the real adventure is the inner expedition to discover a conscious passage to wholeness. Robert is in danger that the Arctic may kill him and his crew. Robert's ego, like his ship, will lack the right ice-breaking equipment, but Victor will arrive as a helpful friend. Robert is literally and figuratively on course to the North Pole, a frozen wasteland of death. He is unaware that the powers of his Self are fully engaged to push his ego elsewhere. The mythic quality of Walton's adventure is that the hero archetype has been activated to confront the sea of the unconscious. The hero's journey imperils his body and ego. Solving the ice problem will be required for Robert's outer and inner lives to survive.

Robert Walton denies the peril of his adventure. He writes to his sister:

"I try in vain to be persuaded that the (North) pole is the seat of frost and desolation; it ever presents itself to my imagination as the region of beauty and delight."

(Letter 1, par 2)

Robert's cheerful attempt to convince his sister not to worry is a thinly-veiled façade covering his fear. His egotistical bravado describes the "delight" of the Arctic. In reality, he is bolstering his courage by denying his instinctual fear of the Arctic cold. Suppressing instincts invites trouble.

When his sister reads these words she experiences the fear that Robert has pushed aside. She assumes his feeling function and worries about the dangers he faces. Robert is a typical man who allows a woman to carry and express his suppressed emotions. The callings of the outer world often require that a man repress his fears and sensitivities. Men have a natural proclivity to find more courage to die in combat than to face the terror of introspection.

"What may not be expected in a country of eternal light?"

(Letter 1, par 2)

Robert's question expresses blind optimism considering it is a December day in northwest Russia that consists of freezing winds and merely dim twilight. Eternal light is a metaphor for the realm of God. Psychologically it connotes his grandiose ego, which experiences itself in a good light. The immature ego is naively identified with the Self, the personal god-image. The young ego sees only its bright side; it cannot see its shadow.

Robert represents the optimistic and courageous young man who has little fear and great confidence in his strength and ability. He is cocksure that he can conquer the challenges of life if he thinks rationally and works diligently.

"These are my enticements, and they are sufficient to conquer all fear of danger and death, and to induce me to commence this laborious voyage with a joy a child feels when he embarks in a little boat....But, supposing all these conjectures to be false, you cannot contest the inestimable benefit which I shall confer on all mankind to the last generation, by discovering a passage near the pole..."

(Letter 1, par 2)

Thus Robert becomes a metaphor for the prototypic analysand, beginning his journey in a state of ego inflation, a little boy in his boat. He feels confident that he'll come to the Arctic, see the passage, and conquer it. Discovering a northwest passage, a technological challenge for the era, fuels his self-aggrandizing expectation to become immortally glorified as a great explorer. He is Prometheus who has stolen fire from the gods. He has also pilfered from the gods an arrogant belief in his divine talent and destiny.

The younger the man the more arrogant he tends to be, but with reasonable cause. Young men have capable and beautiful strong bodies. They enjoy being alive. Their families, women, and neighbors admire them for their athletic prowess. But their humanness eventually catches up to them unless they become like Robert Frost's "an athlete dying young." Julius Caesar gave his arrogant "Veni! Vidi Vici!" speech upon barely conquering Gall, then returned to Rome to be a brutal emperor. We know how Caesar's story ends. Arrogance of youth is a stage in a man's life; but it requires maturation into wisdom of age. Consider my arrogance in this personal dream:

> *Initially I am with four actors comprised of two men and two women in a play. I kill them without remorse. I feel like the Lone Ranger. Next I am on a racetrack driving a 442 cubic inch V-8 powered Oldsmobile circa 1964. I am easily beating the other cars. My inner voice (Self) gets my attention and urges me to evaluate what's going on. It directs me into a cave with a bat. My analyst is there giving a lecture to a group of men. As I reflect on killing the actors I begin to weep.*

The 1964 Oldsmobile 442 was a symbol of machismo (immature male egoism) from my brash high school days. In the dream I am confident because my youthful life is filled with success. The murders without remorse are acts of youthful arrogance. Two men and two women are symbols of the totality of my Self. The *Frankenstein* parallel is that these murdered actors represent potentials that have been excluded by my ego. The journey into the cave has a Batman feeling where the superhero retreats to lick his wounds and reflect. In the cave are unknown men portraying lost characters in my life. I weep, grieving my murdered characters and realizing my immature arrogance. There is a bat flying about the cave, a shadow creature of the night with vampire associations that will be displayed about me later. Bats are scary and may carry dangerous diseases like rabies, but are simultaneously good, eating mosquitoes and flying, i.e., releasing useful libido. Confronting and integrating the shadow is inescapable.

An important detail is the presence of the analyst. When a man begins his midlife inner adventure, he needs a guide. I am led into the cave to join the group who is listening to my analyst guide. The guide of today is usually an analyst. In earlier times he might have been a wise man, a shaman, a priest, or an older family member. In *Frankenstein* Robert has Victor as a wise man and guide.

I am reminded of my own ambitious arrogance. As a young pathologist fresh out residency at Indiana University, I was convinced of my own brilliance and eager to prove my competence. My first position was as a pathologist at Carswell Air Force Base in Fort Worth, Texas. Cocksure, I swaggered about the hospital. I was well trained and the medical staff enthusiastically accepted me professionally and personally. They stroked my ego by expressing what a valuable pathology job I was doing for the surgical services at the hospital.

A mid-life pulmonologist said to me one day. "Greg, you're young and cocky. Reminds me the young lung doctor I was once. Enjoy it while you can." Oblivious to my own hubris, I was insulted. But the middle-aged pulmonologist understood that young men are arrogant. He did not scold or resent me. A Cronus man, consumed with envy and the desire to defend his personal power, would have tried to repress or devour me. The pulmonologist's mid-life transformation allowed him to understand that the time to face my arrogance would come. He knew that I would eventually need to mature beyond this juvenile flaw in my character. Robert Walton's character requires a similar introspective challenge.

Youthful arrogance is abundant at sporting events such as softball, golf, or basketball games. Like my dream image of winning a car race, young men swagger with exaggerated beliefs in their athletic talents. They expect to hit home runs for their softball team, to make baskets in the gym, or to sink putts on the golf course. Too often the slightest failure insults their egos and unleashes immature acts of pouting or golf club tossing. More violent reactions lead to fistfights. Parents and girlfriends shake their heads. They witness the out-of-control retaliation from a bruised ego that we identify with little boys. As time passes their friends and family lose tolerance of their behavior.

> **"I feel my heart glow with an *enthusiasm* (italics added) which elevates me to heaven..."**
>
> **(Letter 1, par 3)**

Enthusiasm means to be inspired or inflated with the divine.

Mythic stories warn of this inflation, best remembered in the story of Icarus who flew so close to the sun god that his wings melted and he crashed to his death. Daedalus, his more mature and humble father, flew lower and was unharmed.

Robert's arrogance of invincibility is dangerous. He is self-absorbed and willing to risk the lives of his crew. Robert's life is on the verge of dissolution. Men commonly come into therapy when their hubris is still intact but their lives are failing. Usually their discontented wives drag them to the therapist's office. Often they refuse the work and quit therapy proclaiming, "It's all bullshit."

When life continues to spiral downward the analysand may return to therapy, particularly when his pain reaches a level that surpasses his denial. He can no longer "handle it." He shakes his head asking, "Why is my job so stupid? Why is my wife such a bitch? Why am I so unhappy; I have everything?"

Robert's first letter explains how he came to inherit his uncle's estate and library. His uncle also passed along a desire for adventure. Robert prepares himself by studying sailing skills necessary for his voyage. He is bent on becoming famous.

"Dear Margaret, do I not deserve to accomplish some great purpose?"

(Letter 1, par 6)

Robert "inherited" his sense for adventure. All men have an innate drive to seek the rough and tumble, our natural rowdy aliveness. It is honest and natural, precious and not pathologic. Prior to maturity, boys use their adventurous energy for their own prosperity or aggrandizement without regard for others.

As part of my adventure I joined the Air Force for selfish, not altruistic reasons. When the draft ended in 1973, the Armed Services were concerned they would be unable to procure physicians. Federal grants to medical students were severely curtailed and I was unwilling to saddle myself with huge loans. I took the bait of an Air Force medical school scholarship purely for the money.

I completed medical school at The University of Illinois, followed by a pathology residency at Indiana University, before serving my military duty of four years. Like Robert Walton investing his inheritance in his adventure, I used the government's money for my own career advancement. I had no animosity for the mission of the Air Force, but in truth I was there purely for my own advancement. This is common. Society praises the ambitious young man who is climbing the corporate ladder, but disdains him if he is profiteering from illegal drug sales. The current generation of MBAs, fresh from graduate school, is constantly looking for the next career advancement. These men have little allegiance to causes other than their own. Several movie characters are good examples of this common feature of young men.

Tom Cruise's title character from *Jerry McGuire* chronicles an athletic agent's transformation from successful self-serving exploitation toward humble and authentic relationships. He becomes disillusioned by his own greed when he identifies it in his girlfriend. Charley Sheen's character in *Wall Street* is a ruthless and criminal stockbroker whose self-serving capacity and immorality lead him to prison. His tragic character is not healed. It ends in vengeance upon an older and even more corrupt corporate executive, Ivan Gekko, played by Micheal Douglas. A third cinematic example of the arrogance of young men is Tom Cruise's character in *Top Gun*. He is a self-serving ace fighter pilot whose personal glory comes before the squadron mission. Men with a priority of personal aggrandizement are "hot-heads." At sporting games their tempers explode easily if they lose.

A man's arrogant ego is notoriously fragile. Just ask a woman. There are two aspects that contribute to this fragility. First, satisfying and sustaining the arrogance of an inflated ego requires a constant input of success to justify the arrogance. A young athlete or golfer must win at any cost because losing would signify that his ego aggrandizement is false. For the tycoon, he must make progressively more money, even if it means destroying companies or committing fraud. The simple reality is that it is humanly impossible to be continuously successful and triumphant.

A common method to validate one's arrogance is to project its need for continuous triumph upon superheroes such as Superman, Michael Jordan, Tiger Woods, or James Bond. Heroes supply the ego its fantasy of supremacy in a feeling-based projective identification. A man doesn't have to admit his own failings because his projection is doing the job. Of course when the idol loses it causes pain to the idolizer's ego. This is why a man takes sports so seriously and becomes angry when his team loses.

The second manifestation of the fragile ego is infantile behavioral outbursts. Reactions of pouting, shouting, or tantrums serve to protect the status of the inflated ego. Pouting and angry outbursts actually soothe the injured ego when its competence cannot be verified. The immature ego suppresses reflection and controls feelings, while the unconscious discharges angry energy. Not having to feel the painful reality of an objective evaluation of the man's true talent protects the ego, and the discharged energy of the tantrum or fight actually enhances the ego's sense of competence.

Mothers, wives and girlfriends are repeatedly bewildered at men who are unable to hear criticisms or tolerate being proved wrong or inadequate. They tire at men's inappropriate assignment of blame when they should acknowledge their own shortcomings. The common joke is that men won't ask for directions. An immature man exhausts extraordinary energy in protecting his fragile ego. Pent-up psychic energy must be dissipated. It is like magma near a crack of the earth's surface. Eventually it will discharge, perhaps as a puff of steam like a tantrum, but it could be a volcano and cause devastation.

The first hurdle a young man must overcome on his path to mature manhood is acknowledging that his ego's investment in grandiosity cannot sustain his life. It is simply too exhausting to maintain a superhero façade. Lois Lane being the exception, no woman on the planet wants to have a relationship with a Superman incapable of defeat.

Abundant empirical data indicate that ego changes occur at predicable ages. Psychological studies, criminal histories, and sociology confirm that men who become severe sociopaths, such as serial killers, are usually in their third to fourth decades. This suggests that the eruptive unleashing of the inner monster for most men peaks during the period from age twenty-five to thirty-five. Men begin in early adulthood, about age twenty-one, to experience the reality of this inner rage. By age twenty-five they become cautious of their inner capacity for rage in response to failure. The auto insurance industry, aware of this age-related male maturation process, reduces rates when men reach twenty-five. Mid-twenties men actively avoid situations that provoke feelings of incompetence, because they have gained some knowledge and fear of their inner capacity to erupt.

Consider another skiing dream from the analysand above who often dreams about skiing situations:

> *The dreamer is skiing and ends up at the bottom of a hill with a slippery concrete culvert. He is unable to climb back up the hill.*

He can not get up the hill. This is deflation of the ego. This man was unsure whether he felt cold, lonely, angry, or depressed. Men commonly are out of touch with and unable to name their emotions. The following is a dream about sub-rosa rage that the dreamer was unaware he had or was expressing in his life. He had no clue why others said he had a short fuse.

> *The dreamer is checking into a hotel. He notices four young men behind a glass enclosed counter who have mean-looking faces. Upon closer examination they are wearing brown shirts with Swastika patches. The dreamer smashes the glass and attacks the Nazi hotel clerks. When he gets into their space behind the counter, they then appear to be mild, normal, and courteous.*

The threat of the Nazis immediately provokes the dreamer's fear and aggression. The hotel, a building of many rooms, is a metaphor for the entire psyche, with areas and staff unrecognizable to the dreamer's ego. Narcissistic rage is represented by the men behind the counter whom he attacks, having projected his inner Nazi upon them. In waking life the man projects inner rage onto family members and co-workers and attacks them. A small-time attack may be throwing golf clubs; big time attack is beating one's wife.

A man in therapy will find fertile ground exploring the inner counterparts to persons he cannot tolerate in the outer world. The above dreamer discovers the unknown hotel clerks to be courteous once he withdraws his Nazi projection and he gets inside their space. This is the diamond-in-the-rough of our monster work.

At mid-life most men begin melting the denial that sustains their grandiosity. When a man discovers the sub-rosa rage that escapes whenever his ego loses its control, it terrifies him that he is unable to prevent the outbursts. Whether punching a hole in the drywall or bruising a lover, the episodes damage relationships, and later remorse fails to remedy the damage. Average men live on high alert to control and stifle their rage. Monster men who make the headlines have deficient rage control.

A collective example was the Bush administration's obsession with "today's terror alert level." Maintaining a state of high vigilance was the Bush administration's way of managing its inner fear of being unable to control society's rage. The administration's over-emphasis on global terrorism was a projection of its anxious desire to control and manipulate. The Bush administration officials spoke of evil men, evil countries, and an "axis of evil." Projecting one's evil is a mechanism to avert the difficult process of recognizing the evil within oneself.

Denial is a method some men use to manage their terror of potentially exploding with rage. They adopt a gentle demeanor to disguise their violent shadows. Many a bride has discovered the sad truth behind her groom's seemingly gentle façade when she becomes a victim of abusive shouting or domestic violence. She is completely at a loss, having not previously seen the monster side of him.

The opposite of denying violent potential is identification. Some men flaunt their inner grandiosity and monster libido. The prisons are teeming with these men who deal drugs, rape, use firearms, steal, and commit violent acts. The grandiosity of criminals allows them to believe they are immune from the consequences of their behaviors.

As men approach forty their adolescent mechanisms to avoid facing their inner monsters fail. Often a bottoming-out event sends a man into therapy or jail or depression. The Tom Cruise character from *Jerry McGuire* loses his job and girlfriend. Other men lose their wives, succumb to alcoholism, or find themselves in legal difficulties. The decision to seek help requires a man to admit that he is suffering and needs assistance. This happened in my life at exactly age 35, when my marriage had become a cesspool of anger.

As a physician I have witnessed many doctors' arrogance crumble when they inadvertently kill a patient or lose a malpractice case. Pete Rose is an example of a man who has never met his monster of grandiosity. His "Charlie Hustle" aggression on the baseball diamond earned him hall-of-fame status, however his violations against league rules proscribing gambling, and his refusal to atone for his violations, prevents his induction. To this day he remains isolated without a relationship to baseball, deprived of his deserved honors, and alone with memories of multiple ex-wives and friends.

NOTES FOR LETTER ONE

1. At some point, typically mid-life, we are all called to an internal adventure: to loosen the control of the ego so that the repressed contents of the unconscious can come into balance.

Question: How have you been called?

2. The ego's ability to control the unconscious wanes as a man reaches mid-life.

Question: What feelings can you no longer control that are causing disruption in your life?

3. Denial, projection, and identification are common modes of ego control.

Question: What has been your main method of maintaining your ego aggrandizement?

4. When a man reaches mid-life he likely will require a mentor or therapist to guide his transition.

Question: Who is available to help you in transition? Do you need to help finding someone?

LETTER TWO

It is March in St. Petersburg and the seas are still frozen. Robert has hired a ship and crew and established his plan to explore the Arctic Sea. The expedition is set to go when the ice permits. Robert experiences an unexpected sense of isolation that he confides to his sister in his second epistle:

> **"But I have one want which I have never yet been able to satisfy; and the absence of the object of which I now feel as a most severe evil. I have no friend, Margaret…"**

(Letter 2, par 2)

Robert is conscious enough to recognize his emptiness and longing for companionship. He goes to the extreme of labeling it evil to ignore the desire longer. Psychologically transgressing the agenda of the Self, the inner god, is an intra-psychic sin. His relationship needs are being carried tenuously in his letter exchanges with his sister, but this fails to satisfy Robert's need for a male friend.

A man disconnected from his relationship function will turn to a woman to supply emotional flow in his life. But a woman is an incomplete replacement for a connection to his male wholeness. Men need male friends because male friends serve as conduits for a man's connection to the masculine aspects of his Self. When a woman carries a man's masculine-toned relationship needs it feels too distant to him. Women sometimes have difficulty understanding why "hanging out" with buddies is so important to men.

When a man exploits a woman's willingness to carry his projected feeling functions, too frequently it becomes sexualized. Sex becomes a ritual conduit for his inner relationship, and instead of moving toward wholeness he feels a schism of emptiness in her absence. A sister, a platonic female friend, or his mother is a more effective processor of a man's feelings than a sexual partner. While having a woman friend is helpful during periods of transition, the tendency to sexualize intimacy has caused many unintended affairs. Freud made a masculine projective error of over-sexualizing emotional feelings.

Freud was wrong that a man wishes to have sex with his mother; a man wishes he could maintain the mother-child arrangement of her processing his feelings.

A corollary to a man's tendency to sexualize intimacy is that when relationship needs are unmet, he may compulsively seek sex. The man feels he can only experience a sense of relatedness during intercourse. His lover may experience this as sexual objectification. She senses accurately that sex with him is depersonalized. His sexual need substitutes for his general need for relationships and his intra-personal need for a relationship with his anima (soul). The woman senses being exploited and she tends to resent the man's requests for sex. Many men acquire compulsive sexual behaviors of viewing pornography or purchasing sexual experiences from prostitutes, in their unconscious search for intra-personal anima connection.

Relatedness is a core desire of a man's soul. In *Frankenstein* the monster carries this unacknowledged desire of Victor Frankenstein; thus the hope for Victor depends upon him establishing a relationship with the monster.

Mythology illustrates the wounded nature of men's desire for relationship. Eros is the male god of love and relationship, an impish son of the disrespected Aphrodite. He sneaks about with a quiver of arrows and mischievously inflicts wounds of amorous passion (Amor). Often Eros is depicted as blind. This relegation of the masculine relationship libido to an infantile prankster indicates that patriarchy has rejected the value of masculine desire and relationship. At a collective level for ten thousand years men have been expected not to attend to relationship desires.

A man with unmet conscious desires is frustrated. But a man with unmet unconscious desires despairs with loss of libido or complete clinical depression.

Healthily Robert Walton is only frustrated because he is able to express his relationship need to his sister. Male authors typically do not create connected relationships for their male characters. They create characters like Captain Ahab, Ulysses, Scrooge, or Ishmael who are essentially alone. Women authors usually write about groups of women and their close relationships: the women of *Pride and Prejudice*, or *Steel Magnolias*, or *Little Women*. In contrast the scientist in Steinbeck's *Cannery Row* lives alone and interacts with a group of male acquaintances down the street. Steinbeck's scientist does demonstrate a deep love and caring for the men, but from a distance. Mary Shelley allows Robert to feel his need for male friendship.

Some Darwinists argue that it was necessary for younger men to be detached from their relationship functions; that *Homo sapiens* survival required warriors to protect the tribe. If men had compassion for the enemy or too much sensitivity against warfare, the tribe would be in peril.

Men experience partial relationship needs through camaraderie in bars, playing softball, or fishing. These are activity-based friendships that satisfy masculine affiliation needs, but these friendships generally fail to adequately meet a man's deeper needs for the soul's totality. What superficial male relationships lack is a rich sense of emotion, particularly the feminine-toned soul-mate, a one-on-one friendship, the type of friend that Robert Walton wishes to have.

Consider this dream about a man's need for a deep friendship:

> *The dreamer is in Chicago near the lake. He is with his best friend from college. They notice an unimproved lot at 1000 N Lakeshore, an unbelievable site for a house and a phenomenal value. The hook is that another man, a law student acquaintance of the dreamer has the purchase rights to the property. To the horror of the dreamer, his college friend throws the law student over an embankment and presumably kills him. The house is built, but when completed the dreamer notices that his half of the lot is completely barren of landscaping, while the college friend's half has abundant vegetation. The dreamer feels his side of the house is cursed due to the murder of the law student. He gets a flashlight and searches the area under an embankment next to the lot. He discovers the law student who is still alive and not angry. Once freed, the law student is happy.*

The dreamer's unconscious is barren because the best friend (ego) only meets half the needs of the dreamer's total psyche. Lacking in his life is a relationship with the law student to fulfill needs of discarded parts of his unconscious. The law student, who represents the power of the shadow, is entitled to own and live in part of the house. In psychotherapy the dreamer must accept that he has excluded (killed) a part of himself responsible for his half-barren landscape. The spot by the lake (near the unconscious waters) is ideal and the completion of the house (individuation) is a phenomenal value, but this requires inclusion of his law student. Notice how evil/murderous the ego is about refusing to include the other friend.

I spent years in which my only male friends were golfing and drinking partners. During the winter months we would never see one another. Even when we played golf, the conversation did not include items other than golf, sports, or politics. These are the topics familiar to men because they limit conversation to worldly war stories. Emptiness persists in shallow relationships, because men fail to touch the depths of their souls. Ritual drinking, jokes, and womanizing often define the ineffective and shallow relationships that leave men pining for deeper soul bonding. Often after a golf outing, while sipping beers, a predictable subset of the men will gather recruits to visit a strip club. These men become uncomfortable with conversation and compulsively seek a ritual sexual escape to the feminine to manage the emptiness of inadequate relatedness.

The exception in my life was a softball team that regularly sipped post-game beers in the parking lot while discussing parenting, their loves, careers, religion, and philosophy. This group was different because the men were older (35-55), educated, and the group leaders included clergy and men who had been through mid-life therapy.

Most men are stoic and do not engage easily. An eighty-year-old friend, who is gregarious and adept at conversation, talks easily with strangers on the street about the pleasantries such as the weather. But whenever I attempt to engage him in a feeling based exchange, I hit a brick wall. Men of his era, WWII's Greatest Generation, believe "real men" avoid feelings. In contrast their children, "the baby boomers," began a "men's movement" in the late 80's when they hit midlife, specifically for feeling based interactions. The women laughed at these men who gathered in the woods to beat drums and read poetry. I attended such meetings for several years. The forum provided a ritual space where feeling-based talk was protected and expected. The men who attended these gatherings had enough desire for deeper masculine relationships that they endured the ridicule. They were seeking feeling-toned relationships missing in their lives.

At midlife, the soul of a man demands integration. If a man is ready to engage his soul, he will become a seeker. If he is unwilling to submit to the demands of his soul and remains unconscious, he may perform silly midlife acts: dressing like a twenty-year-old, taking on a young girlfriend, or buying a red sports car. These events of his "mid-life" crisis are side steps from the inner journey to wholeness.

Dreams that depict a man searching for a lost friend, or father, or co-worker are callings toward wholeness. The lakeside dreamer is pushed to befriend the law with a flashlight: turning on the lights is a common dream metaphor for inner discovery.

Often when a man begins therapy, simultaneously a new friend "appears" synchronistically to assist the mid-life transitional adventure. Seemingly out of the blue a mentor appears who causes the relationship function of a man to germinate. Some men, particularly those with abusive father figures, can only trust their stories to a woman because for them adult men are too toxic to trust. Men's groups that meet specifically for the purpose of sharing feelings are an excellent venue to recommend to analysands who express a need to explore relationships with other men. Pushing men, who have not expressed friendship needs, into relationships rarely is successful. These men are too out of touch with their needs for male friendships to accept the suggestion.

Robert Walton's letter to his sister asking for a friend is like a prayer to the gods. The gods respond, delivering Victor Frankenstein to his ship.

Robert has an egocentrism typical for an immature man. His desire for friendship is essentially selfish, i.e., he wants to feel better more than a sharing exchange. He tells his sister he wants someone to witness the glory and excitement of his adventure. Women know about dealing with the narcissism of a twenty-something man. A man directs conversation to: his job, his athletic achievements, his health, and his ambitions. Social plans are difficult because the gratification of the man greatly overshadows his ability to stretch to accommodate his woman friend. "I ain't going to a chick flick." Or, "I would never change a diaper." These types of responses achieve two goals: selfish pleasure and maintaining a "manly" façade.

The narcissistic façade is a defensive posture to protect a fragile ego from being shamed by the outside world. Is he good enough? Is he succeeding? Does he have value in the eyes of others? When a man's libido is fully engaged in outer competition, it results in disconnection with his feelings. He is also disconnected from the feelings of others, who see him as narcissistic.

The arrogance and narcissism of youth is an inherent stage of development that must be tolerated, annoying as it is. Nagging and bitching from his wife will not improve their relationship problems. Shaming and humiliation will make the relationship worse or even dangerous. Before she can engage him, the young man must learn to connect with his own neglected feelings.

An older male mentor is probably the person best capable of introducing a man to his narcissism without pathologizing its presence. Patience and encouragement are needed, but also timeliness. Waiting too long risks the danger that his monster will be provoked into revenge for the shaming attacks. An important problem of modern American society is that it offers little encouragement for a man seeking to reconnect with his soul. Men are culturally shamed for their "mid-life crises."

Robert tells his sister of his wish for acceptance:

> **"I desire the company of a man who could sympathize with me; whose eyes would reply to mine."**
>
> **(Letter 2, par. 2)**

"Eyes that reply" is a poetic expression for mirroring, feedback that validates a man's emotions. What a great gift to have a friend who sees and understands you. Robert feels a macho shame associated with his request for a friend. He disparages himself for inadequate education, but his real fear is humiliation of being judged un-masculine for his relationship needs:

> **"Now I am twenty-eight, and am in reality more illiterate than many schoolboys of fifteen…(still)…I greatly need a friend who would have a sense not to despise me as**

> romantic, and affection enough for me to regulate my
> mind."

(Letter 2, par. 2)

This is the rub in the ointment of therapy for many men: it makes them feel sappy and unmasculine. Hence many men simply cut and run when confronted with doing therapy, preferring a shot of bourbon and tickets to a boxing match.

Robert is receptive to accepting a mentor, the right one who will appreciate his romanticism. He seeks a mentor because granting himself permission to be romantic is too difficult for his current ego. Collective psychic health requires a cultural acceptance of these difficult passages for men. Gail Sheehy has written two excellent books about how men process transition: *New Passages* (1977) and *Understanding Men's Passages* (1998) by Thorndike Press.

Carl Jung believed that the first half of a man's life demands gaining success in the outer world to establish career, wife, and family. The task of the second half begins at mid-life to achieve individuation by gaining a mature integration of his entire psyche. The sequence proceeds through stages from independence, to self-awareness, and finally to inter-relatedness. Independence means separation from the influence of parents and culture, and withdrawing projections of shadow contents from others. Self-awareness is the acquisition of knowledge about one's psychic complexity. It requires personal permission to be authentic. Inter-dependence is a re-connecting with the outer world from a new conscious position of differentiated uniqueness.

Walton's second letter introduces a hopeful image of an individuated man. He describes the crew-master, whom Robert hires because he has a kind heart, the antithesis of a stereotypical brutal seaman.

> "The master is a person of an excellent disposition, and is remarkable in the ship for his gentleness and the mildness of his discipline."

(Letter 2, par. 4)

The crew-master's story exemplifies mature love. He loved a young Russian lady of moderate fortune. Her father arranged a wedding between his daughter and the crew-master. Just before the wedding, the woman, bereft in tears, threw herself at the crew-master's feet and pleaded for his mercy. She confessed a love for another man who was so poor that her father refused to consent to their marriage. Moved, the crew-master expressed his unselfish regard for her happiness and revoked their engagement. Further, he gave her his farm and livestock that he had purchased in anticipation of his own marriage to her. He then solicited her father's consent to allow her to marry the young man whom she loved. The father refused on grounds of honor to his agreement. The crew-master, finding the father impossibly resolute, left the country vowing never to return until the woman was married according to her wishes.

The crew-master's story is a hopeful tale of rejecting patriarchal oppression. The crew-master is not obsessed with power and narcissism. He can see women as separate persons and not as property. Finally he promotes the greater good by giving away his farm. The crew-master's character offers dramatic hope for Robert Walton's maturation. Can Robert master managing his inner crew of psychic characters with wisdom and compassion?

A key aspect of the crew-master's authenticity is a mature feeling function that allows the flow of his soul. It has a strong masculine tone. The successes of men's groups are substantially the result of presenting masculine men as role models for carrying a mature feeling function. Robert Bly is embraced widely by men. His book, *Iron John*, is recommended for teaching men about masculine feelings. Mentors, like the crew-master, allow men to experience the flow of feeling in another man so that they are able to access it in themselves.

The unconscious man initially feels disdain or even hatred for other men who exhibit feelings. A young man will hate or ridicule "sappy" old men before he will admire and long to experience an older man's joy of living. But when a man's envy dissolves and he becomes a mid-life seeker, he may follow the older man about as a new puppy clings to his owner. As an Air Force captain, I and other younger doctors avoided socializing with the senior officers and doctors. We busied ourselves treating patients and actively excluded our older colleagues. Ten years later in private practice, I was spending two-hour lunches with doctors nearing retirement, hungry to hear their stories of life.

Obviously, not all men mature toward mid-life seeking older men to assist their maturation. Many regress to a renewed adolescence. A typical regression is observed in forty-year-old divorced men looking for twenty-something women who are young-enough and willing-enough to carry a man's anima projection. Meanwhile their forty-year-old ex-wives tend to prefer fifty-something men for the opposite reason. The women want a man who has developed the capacity to carry his own feminine parts. Despite the current TV "cougarism," most forty-plus women are repelled by the narcissism of younger men and are more attracted to older men.

Robert's second letter to his sister concludes with:

"There is something at work in my soul which I do not understand."

(Letter 2, par. 6)

The line conveys the autonomous nature of the Self's push toward wholeness. The line also has a quality of trepidation because Robert intuits that his Self includes monstrous aspects of his totality that can become irrepressible.

At age thirty-four I left the Air Force and moved to central Indiana to begin my permanent job as a pathologist. The first several years I was busy establishing my career at the hospital. My home life was typical with the challenges of parenting two small daughters and being a good-enough-husband to an attorney wife who also was struggling to juggle family and career. Yet as age thirty-five approached I had an unshakable awareness that an inner discontent was growing like a tumor inside me.

My medical practice was prosperous and the American dream was mine, however, contentment was missing. The new house, car, and boat failed to relieve my emptiness. My relationship with my wife had gone sour. We argued incessantly about parenting and politics. No activity or purchase was gave me joy. I was becoming cold and numb without zest for life.

While building a new house, my wife and I spent four days bickering about which shingles to purchase. This was a suffocating torture for me. I wondered how my life had come to such joyless drudgery. Success had become a Midas touch. Material possessions brought maintenance and resentment. I rued my education as a waste of my youth, feeling I had squandered it studying while my friends were enjoying sports and parties. My world was gray and meaningless. I had become a lonely polar bear trapped on an ice floe in the Arctic. My discontent meant I was out of touch with the true desires of my soul.

NOTES FOR LETTER TWO

1. Jung considered the purpose of the first half of life is to establish a position in the outer world, the second is to reconcile with the inner world.

Question: What has ended in your life? Become stale? Or changed from very important to insignificant?

2. The transition of mid-life is a natural age-predictable experience. It is heralded when a man is called by an inner desire for wholeness.

Question: What obsessive thoughts, needs, or feelings are recurring to you that you cannot get out of your mind?

3. A mentor is sought and usually necessary. Choose a mentor who has been "through it."

Question: Who is an older man in your life that you feel understands the journey you are undertaking because he has been through it?

4. READ! A man is not alone and the stories from other men's transitions will make him feel less crazy. The images in books will help loosen the lug nuts for the tires (tired old ways) that need changing. The appendix of cited books is a good starting library.

5. Seek and develop relationships with men.

Question: Can you name two men with whom you feel you can connect with beyond the superficial?

LETTER THREE

It is July and the ship is sailing full speed. Robert ignores the menacing icebergs, as does the crew. To disregard warning signs while forging ahead on the same path is a common mistake of neglecting one's instinctual needs. Such is the man who works constantly and avoids his wife and children. Visions of success make Robert oblivious to the perilous nature of both his sea adventure and his restless soul.

LETTER FOUR

On July 31st the crew sights an ice floe carrying an eight-foot humanoid creature traveling by sled. The last of July is symbolic, a metaphor for the early second half of life, the time for mid-life transition. Sighting the monster on the sled is Walton's first inclination that monsters are real. Experiencing the closeness of the Frankenstein monster disturbs him, a precursor terror of meeting his own monster. This inner transition begins by seeing in another that which is invisible in the mirror, and being uncomfortably moved by the image. He has not achieved the wisdom of Shakespeare that *"the fault, dear Brutus, lies not in our stars, but within ourselves."*

    The next morning the ship's crew sights Victor Frankenstein's sled lagging a few hours behind in pursuit of the monster. The crew rescues Victor and brings him onboard. Only one dog is alive from Victor's sled team, a metaphor that Victor is down to the end of his animal resources. Intra-psychically this is the final breath of his inner spirit.

The mad-eyed and disheveled Victor appears cadaverous but responds spasmodically to Robert's kindness. This captivates and enchants Robert. In psychological parlance, Robert experiences positive transference; unconsciously bonding to Victor who will serve to mentor his soul's encounter.

An old saw of psychotherapy is that when the analysand is ready, the mentor will come. Two ways of framing this idea include: first, a metaphysical faith that one's god or guardian angel is there at the time of need. The second approach, a psychological framing, is that the Self is constantly scanning the environment to latch onto an appropriate conduit for its agenda. Combining the explanations yields: the Self, the inner god-image, finds us a mentor.

Despite Robert Walton's gracious treatment, Frankenstein cannot overcome his despair. Frankenstein is only interested in his monster, the "daemon." Daemon means god-like spirit and connotes a person's instinctual aspects. Author Philip Pullman has written a children's book series, *The Dark Matter*, in which each person has a visible animal daemon that follows them around and talks to them. This is a wonderful image of the natural soul of a person. Unfortunately the world's major religions have a pejorative and satanic view of instinctual desires imaged in the daemon spirit. Judeo-Christian tradition has split-off and banished the inner spirit and libido parts of humans and in the process changed the spelling of daemon to the satanic spelling of demon. This religious demonization of the animal, sexual, and intuitive aspects means equating them with sin and Satan. In cultures prior to monotheisms, daemons were not evil and carried a wealth of good libido. Satan has psychologically been separated from the all-good-god in heaven and relegated to the all-evil-devil in hell. *Frankenstein* shows that denial of parts carried by our daemons will bring hell upon us. The opposite of the daemon from hell is the angel from heaven; Robert feels his prayers for life have been answered in Victor Frankenstein.

Robert writes:

> **"I begin to love him as a brother; and his constant and
> deep grief fills me with sympathy and compassion,"**
>
> (Letter 4, par. 20)

The path to wholeness begins when we welcome the inner wretch as a family member and honor its life. Acknowledging Victor's sadness initiates the flow of Robert's feelings. Robert refers to Victor as "the stranger." Victor is Robert's internal stranger as he receives projections from Robert. Robert reveals his dreams of discovering a northwest passage, but is disappointed when Victor fails to share his excitement. Victor is livid and warns Robert to abandon his quest. He invites Robert to hear his monster tale. The prologue is thus completed and Victor begins the monster story, hoping it will inspire Robert's salvation:

> **"I do not know that the relation of my disasters will be
> useful to you; yet, when I reflect that you are pursuing
> the same course, exposing yourself to the same dangers
> which have rendered me what I am, I imagine that you
> may deduce an apt moral from my tale."**
>
> (Letter 4, par. 31)

NOTES FOR LETTER FOUR

1. An early event in a man's transition to maturity is the introduction of the monster, or destructive shadow. A man often first discovers monsters in others.

Question: Can you describe an ugly shadow of another person and then identify how a part of him is like you?

2. The daemon spirit possesses an animalistic instinctual libido. It likely has both good and evil potentials. The moral outcome of the

daemon's expression is determined by the extent that the ego can constructively integrate the daemon's libido.

Question: Can you identify a good and an evil impulse in your shadow such as lust, greed, creativity, power, softness, etc., that you cannot currently act out?

CHAPTER 1

Victor's tale begins like an initial therapy session as he lays out his family's back-story. He was born into a well-to-do Swiss family with two wonderful parents. Most analysands come to therapy with a belief that they had typical childhoods with minimal problems. In reality most of us come from homes with closets full of dysfunctional ancestors and abusive child-rearing practices.

We all were traumatized, whether in major or minor ways. With a major issue of emotional trauma, the first item in therapy is detoxification. A victim of physical or sexual abuse, traumatic stress, addiction, or a social malady such as poverty, religious fundamentalism, or war, must be eased out of the toxic state of fear and defense. A person cannot engage in effective therapy while in a state of hypervigilant fear.

Fortunately for Victor Frankenstein, he was spared major trauma in childhood. His father was a good provider. His mother was attentive, nurturing, pleasant, and loving: a paragon of kindness. He enjoyed a childhood filled with play and happiness. Birth order enthusiasts will recognize Victor as a prototypical first-born who received parental doting known only to oldest children who experience undivided parental attention before the arrival of subsequent siblings. He is predictably self-assured and courageous when he ventures out into the world. Like first-borns, Victor has a strong inclination and willingness to submit to parental expectations:

> **"I was their plaything and their idol, and something better-their child, the innocent and helpless creature bestowed on them by Heaven, whom to bring up to good, and whose future lot it was in their hands to direct to happiness or misery, according as they fulfilled their duties towards me."**

(Chap 1, par 7)

Also typical of first-borns, he will find it difficult to overcome parental expectations and introjects. Victor accepts his culture's belief that parents have the duty and province to shape their children. This belief, unquestioned by Victor's parents, is rampant worldwide. A curse of world religions is the command for parents to confiscate their child's soul. A man's transformation requires self-permission to change imposed attitudes that are incongruent with his Self. This permission cannot and will not come from others. The analysand will likely be condemned by those invested in the cultural hierarchy. Permission cannot be obtained simply through the performance of rituals or chanting affirmations. This is a monumental task that may require years. The more intense the parental love, the more difficult it is to gain self-permission to change.

The basis of depth psychology is that an individual has a right to a personal life unlike most religious doctrine that grant individuals no intrinsic value other than achieving worthiness by executing a holy agenda. The holy agenda invariably comes from a priest, caliph, or other prophetic administrator. The "scriptures" are an external prescription, (pre-written) for the masses and from the individual. Common religious traditions do not support following and developing an individual's agenda of the Self. A jihadist's directive to a young man to become a suicide bomber on behalf of Allah is a frightening example of the concept of external prescription.

A child is too immature physically and psychologically to combat the extrinsic forces of parents and culture. A child's psyche cannot assert any meaningful individual Self-agenda. The psychic process of individuation is a life-long uphill struggle. One cannot succeed without summoning the courage to defy parental, religious, and cultural forces.

In fairness cultural goals are altruistic, striving to produce good citizens. Parents wish their children to cooperate with society and not to scare the bejeezus out of their neighbors. However, from an individual psychological perspective, the introjections of societal and parental agendas cause substantial psychic blockage. Anxiety, depression, and inadequate self-esteem are injuries that result from a blocked evolution of one's Self. Suicide can be an active end to these injuries when the ego can see no pathway to expression.

Suppression of the Self's totality may manifest as a dangerous intra-psychic pressure that can provoke violence. This is a central tenant of this book: that transformation of monster potentials requires the acceptance of individual psychic needs.

Following the agenda of one's Self and co-existing with family and neighbors is a perpetual existential dilemma. Depth psychology does not suggest we abandon parenting and religious instruction. It asks that the individual Self of each person be respected and nourished. Cultures use elaborate rituals and education to mold children into productive citizens. Social order would collapse in its absence, but the essence of ritual is to advance a societal agenda and to overcome the drives of the individual. Cultural duty often violates the individuality of its members. Creating a balance in one's life between cultural expectations and one's uniqueness is an unpleasant but essential psychic task. It is not a volunteer assignment that we can avoid.

Society is terrified of individual needs. When society rebukes unacceptable parts a of a person's psyche those parts are sent to the shadow reservoir to become libido of the inner monster. The monster-making potential of even the kindest of parents is present in Shelley's words: "as they direct to happiness or misery." Misery will drive the monster.

Each character of the novel is a metaphor for Victor's relationship with an archetype. First is Victor's mother, she represents the mother-complex. From birth a mother carries her son's feminine-toned feeling function that organizes his emotions. Jungians name this feminine-toned feeling organizer the anima archetype.

Like most mothers Caroline Frankenstein is attentive to her child's needs. When a mother interprets her child's hunger, anger, curiosity, or happiness, she is performing his feeling function for him. She appropriately responds to his cries as a nurturing servant. The child develops a process that relegates emotional or feeling states to his mother's care. Mother becomes an accessory structure of a boy's psyche, like the placenta is a physical accessory organ to the fetus. The downside to her success is that her son feels little need to develop a conscious personal system of emotional processing and self-nurturing. Boys grow into manhood with deficient feeling functions, consequently too many adult men remain too attached to their mothers.

Victor's mother models the good mother. She has the kind habit of visiting poor families and bestowing generosity. Caroline Frankenstein's inspiration is in part genuine caring and in part *noblesse oblige*. Shelley has given her the name of Caroline. Carol is a Christian song of praise, particularly a Christmas song. Victor's mother is a sweet true Christian woman in word and deed. Phonetically it sounds like "care all," the task of the great, collective mother. Caroline also is a diminutive feminine derivative of the name, Charles, meaning full grown and adult.

Caroline's maiden surname is Beaufort. Literally translated it means a fort of the boy; a psychological metaphor of a force guarding his emotions. A beau is not just any boy, but connotes a dandy, or naive male suitor. Beaufort well describes the psychological function of the mother as an early guard of a boy's inner feminine.

Women instinctively allow themselves to become feeling carriers for boys. When a mother brings her five-year-old son into work, other women surround the boy and make him feel like an all-important prince. They talk softly and excitedly about his clothes and toys. They praise him for helping his mother. They tell him how smart and cute he is. Women fall naturally into the role of emotional organizer for boys. This fawning is warm and nurturing to the boy. Mother's doting is not harmful, but the boy will need to shed it like a snakeskin in order to mature.

Maturing through the mother-complex requires two achievements. First, the boy must separate physically from the mother's space so that he can independently experience the world. The second task, a Herculean endeavor, is that a young man must mature his internal emotional organizing function, his anima, to function independently from his mother and later from his wife. The symbiotic "mommy's boy" is a man who achieves inadequate emotional independence from his mother.

Few boys want to grow up and leave the comfort of their mothers. What about dad? As fathers become better nurturers, they share with mothers the task of carrying their son's feeling function. But sons with two carriers of their feeling function have no guarantee of less difficulty in achieving parental detachment. Hollywood recently illustrated this theme in the movie, *Failure to Launch*. The story concerns a man in his thirties too comfortable to leave his parents' home. The ultimate reason a man develops his own emotional processing is to become an authentic individual.

The mother-complex manifests as a set of unconscious feelings, emotions, and anxieties associated with one's mother. Projection occurs when a boy allows his mother to name, to process, and to organize his emotions. Introjection occurs when the mother instills into him, her program for organizing his emotions.

Envision a common playground incident: a boy shoves another boy to the ground. The victim begins crying. His mother arrives and identifies a cut knee. She acknowledges the pain and delivers comfort. Next she assuages his anger at the other boy by labeling the shove a "mean thing to do." She praises her son for not hitting back. The son's emotions concerning the incident are projected upon his mother outside and processed by her outside of his psyche.

The mother introjects the idea into her son that he is good because he did not retaliate. If an instinctual part of the boy felt the need to retaliate against the perpetrator, then that energy must go somewhere. Where? Into his shadow! It is stowed as a libidinous potential for retribution at a later time. But how can that retaliation energy be retrieved if the mother has introjected a guiding principle that nice boys don't hit back? This boy will have recurring anxiety whenever feelings of aggression rise within him. Anxiety associated with retaliation or aggression becomes a symptom of his mother-complex.

Caroline Beaufort is a loving mother, but she complies with the established patriarchy. When Caroline's father was dying, she nursed him continuously for nine months, an image of serving the patriarchy. A good friend and financial supporter of Caroline's father was Alfonse Frankenstein who took pity on the poverty-stricken Caroline. Seeing Caroline weep upon her father's coffin, he offered to care for her in his home. Despite Alfonse being much older, they married two years later. Caroline's devotion to her dying father and then coupling with his friend is a metaphor for feminine submission to the patriarchy. The image of Caroline crying over her father's coffin is an important detail for later discussion.

A man's mother-complex is a murky mixture of personal mother and "Great Mother." The Great Mother refers to the collective archetype that includes the forces of Mother Nature, especially birth and death. Collective relationships within a church and society are also feminine-toned and act unconsciously to control and alter emotional states. The expression of a particular man's mother-complex may take any of a variety of patterns.

The most common, the ideal mother-complex, is exampled in Victor Frankenstein. He has an "ideal mother." His mother is sweet and seemingly perfect. Such a son grows up believing that his mother and women are the ultimate in caring. They also unconsciously believe processing emotions is women's work, because they are good at it, it is the natural order, and men shouldn't even try, thus pushing the feeling function into his shadow.

The ideal mother is the mother image that is revered on Mother's Day or the image we see when watching TV and a three-hundred-pound football player on the screen smiles, waves, and mouths the words, "Hi, Mom." We assume she has provided kind and helpful support the young man, but we also intuit that he subjugates feeling function to his mother, as he turns to her in his moment of elation.

Consider this man's dream:

> The dreamer is at an amusement park and sees an old naked woman in a carnival dunking booth. Bert Parks is the emcee who places the woman atop a huge balloon figure of Paul Bunyan that moves robotically.

The old woman is the dreamer's mother-complex: helpless, naked, and exploited in a carnival setting. Parks, the perennial host of the Miss America Pageant, represents the patriarchy's sexual exploitation of women. Beauty pageants perpetuate patriarchal control by encouraging young women to aspire to become sex objects and servants of men.

The key to this dream is that the woman is placed atop the mythical "man" of Paul Bunyan, a cartoonish mythical folk hero. As a balloon he is phony and puffed up, a description of patriarchal grandiosity. He moves robotically as an inhuman drone of the patriarchy. Psychologically this is equivalent to saying the dreamer is participating in a carnival where he is a puffy fake man and his feminine side (the female image of the old woman) is being humiliated or drowned.

In life the dreamer is a man who gives patriarchal homage to his mother. He holds his mother and women in regard, but only when they conform to cultural ideals. This type of mother-complex, the patriarchal ideal mother, is expressed by the man who must keep his wife at home to maintain his sense of manhood.

A different type of over-idealized mother is the "powerful mother." This type of mother-complex is pervasive among men raised by single parent mothers or in households where the mother holds total power. These sons tend to over-identify with the power of women. They desire to please their mothers, which saps their ability to negotiate with them, and subsequently with women in general. These sons project their power onto, and inevitably come to resent women. President Clinton had this type of mother. He married a strong woman like his mother, but he also engaged in sexual exploits over younger less empowered women, a shadow aspect of this type of mother-complex. Power abdicated to a woman makes the man feel inadequate and diminished; it also activates a desire to exploit or hurt her in retaliation.

Common dream motifs for men struggling with a powerful mother-complex include being watched or discovered by their mothers during sex. Men with the powerful mother-complex commonly experience a pervasive sense of shame when judged by women. Any woman can evoke in him a terror of losing face. She may be his wife, girlfriend, mother, or co-worker.

A surgical colleague gave me this dream:

The dreamer is a doctor helping a neurosurgeon to operate on the medulla of a girl with Down syndrome. The doctor gets confused and cuts up her nerves. He then goes to the waiting room to explain to her mother that he screwed up and that her daughter is dead.

The Down syndrome girl symbolizes the state of the dreamer's personal anima. She is deformed and retarded in development. The doctor wants to cure her retarded state, which is the same as saying he wants to mature his feminine side. He is working on the deepest level of the brain to awaken her, the medulla that controls the sleep centers of the brain. This image implies that the necessary operation (transformation of his psyche) is a life or death issue. He does not have the ability to perform the operation; therefore, he needs the neurosurgeon to assist. He is confused and the process leads to failure. He feels shame in facing the girl's mother. This man has an idealized and critical mother image that has control over his feminine emotions. He waits in terror to receive shame from a mother figure. Overcoming his loss of power, i.e., healing his shame associated with is mother-complex, is necessary for this man to move forward.

The power issue in mother-complex work often results from dysfunctional bonding between mother and son that is evident in the son's adult relationships. Ideally, a mother provides enough closeness to make her son feel secure and loved, while maintaining enough separation so that he can mature and fully experience the world. But ideal mothers rarely exist. To some extent the real mother either remains too close to her son or she abandons the boy by not relating to him.

In the latter case when a man has an emotionally unavailable mother, he may respond by becoming an adult with no ability to trust or relate to women. If he does marry, it is to a woman who can tolerate his cold and suspicious treatment of her. Other times this man will become a flyboy, a Peter Pan, who is so unconsciously fearful of bonding with a woman that he compulsively runs from relationships.

Some men develop a mother-complex of over-idealization because they received too little mothering. Particularly prone are those who experienced the loss of their natural mothers in childhood from death or divorce. They overcompensate with clinging neediness to their women partners, feeling like a two-year-old left with a baby-sitter when they are alone. "Pussy-whipped" men have immense difficulty in negotiating life issues with their women partners.

A variant of not getting enough satisfying mothering can manifest in the "contemptuous" mother-complex. This mother ignored and devalued her son's feelings which activated resentment in her son's shadow. Consider the story of Daryl who had a combative relationship with his mother. She was sickly and demanded Daryl's attention and servitude. She began sentences with phrases such as "Get me..." and "I want..." As a young boy Daryl resented not receiving enough personal attention. After marrying he soon began fighting with his wife for no apparent reason. Daryl's history is a litany of political strife and confrontations. His relationships end in verbal combat. Wherever he feels bonded, Daryl engages in verbal combat.

Daryl entered therapy when his mother became terminally ill. Daryl visited her regularly, but the battles continued as conversations erupted into arguments. The arguments were outwardly trivial and inane. Daryl visited at the wrong time. Mother did not care about Daryl's job. Daryl's neglect of her has caused her cancer. The underlying conflict arose from Daryl's mother's demands for servitude and Daryl's need for his mother to steward his emotions. Her failure to meet his childhood needs left him with a festering wound. For Daryl any deep sense of feeling connection with a woman is accompanied by an immediate urge to engage in verbal combat, an unconscious expression of his rage with his mother. Daryl refuses to accept that he has contemptuous mother-complex issues. He resists his therapist's attempts to have him reflect on the possibility.

Unlike Daryl's mother who refused to connect with her son's anima, "the warden" mother over-controls the anima of her son. This "imperialistic" mother-complex occurs when the mother captures her son's anima and imprisons it in her psyche unattended. Her agenda is to stifle her son's independence. The son's emotions are frozen within his mother and the son becomes numb. He has no sense that his feelings are important. What little emotional processing she offers is token and insincere to placate him. Her smile and reassurance leaves him detached from his actual emotions. As his emotions have never been adequately modulated, this type of man reaches adulthood stiff and unable to experience feelings.

The "inadequate" mother-complex involves a mother who impotently but excessively smothers her son with affection. She has the best of intentions but just isn't up to the task of genuinely stewarding his feelings. She is frozen and often without the flow of her own genuine emotional process. Lacking an empathic base she fakes her understanding of the boy, but her son knows she is faking. He cannot trust her ability to process his emotional projections and eventually resents her inability to carry his feeling function. This boy misses the opportunity to have assistance for his emotional processing. This doting mother is not controlling like the "warden mother" who withholds emotional modulation; the "inadequate mother" has nothing to offer.

The "exploitive mother" trades love for manipulation. She understands her son's emotions, but uses them to control his behavior according to her agenda. Consider Sol. His father died when he was eleven. His mother is known as the gentlest and kindest of women except by her own child. Sol's experience of his mother was that she demanded to know everything: Where did he go and with whom? Did he shower after soccer? Who was his girlfriend? Did he wash his hands? Did he do his essay, and did he proofread it? It's a common drill re-enacted by today's over-involved parents and encouraged by the baby-boomer culture who believes the "right" toys, books, pre-school, friends, etc. will allow them to mold their children. Sol's exploitative mother is quick to interpret his emotions and attempts to introject her agenda in response to any action or activity by her son. Many of today's young adults seem to lack purpose and ambition because their parents have poisoned the water in the pond of their child's true desire. A person who has missed the experience of genuine personal desire feels life is boring and meaningless.

Sol came to associate the feminine with feeling entrapped. Consequently after college he left his home state never to return. So toxic is his feeling side that he married a woman who promised to forego having children. Sol did not want to have children for two reasons: first, to avoid reliving the toxic feelings of his smothering childhood; and second, to inflict revenge upon his mother who desires grandchildren. Sol's mother-image evokes guilt and anger. The therapeutic challenge for Sol is to arrange a prison break for his anima.

The mothers above are lovable human beings. They tried their best. Neighbors and friends testify truthfully that they were wonderful parents. The point is that every man has a mother who has impacted the feminine side of his psyche. A mature man must accept that his mother did her best and cease blaming her as a person for his mother-complex issues. He must take responsibility for separating his internal emotional organization from the influence of his mother.

Victor Frankenstein, as does any man, has mother-complex work to do. His ideal mother is a tad too perfect; thus Victor can never live up to her standards. His first step is to recognize that he is not like his mother, not required to act like her, not required to think like her, nor required to execute her agenda

A roadblock for Victor in rejecting his mother's agenda is his idealizing love for her. The most insidious of his mother's requests is to marry the family's adopted daughter, Elizabeth: his adopted sister, for God's sake! Victor's therapist must assure him that denying the request will not be the end of the world. He should expect a blank stare when he asks Victor whether he has emotionally processed the prospect of marrying Elizabeth. Predictably a man like Victor will have difficulty believing his mother's agenda may not represent his true desire.

An example of this occurs when men go shopping. The man finds a sweater to purchase that he thinks is attractive. He holds it up to his wife and says, "I like this red sweater." His wife rolls her eyes and says, "Don't you like this blue one better?" Not only does he immediately agree with his wife and buys the blue sweater, but he comes to believe the red sweater is ugly. His malleability, an example of introjected emotional organization, results from idealizing a woman's opinion.

Victor unquestioningly acquiesces to his mother's suggestions. An interesting historical aside is that Sir Francis Beaufort in 1808 (Shelley's England) was an engineering celebrity in London. During the heyday of English sea superiority, Beaufort devised the Beaufort wind force scale system for sailing navigation. Caroline Beaufort navigated the waters of feeling (the anima) for her son, and finding Victor a sister-wife was a psychic sea victory over Victor's anima.

How did Caroline procure Victor's future wife? During one of Caroline's many trips to Milan to give alms to the poor, she visited a destitute widow with several children. One girl, named Elizabeth, instantly attracted the attention of Victor's mother, who longed for a daughter. Unlike the other children, Elizabeth had delicate features and blonde hair because she was an orphan of German parents. Feeling sorry for the impoverished family, Victor's mother convinced the Milanese woman to lessen the family's penury by offering to adopt her. Caroline described Elizabeth as "a present" to Victor. People remarked on the striking resemblance between Elizabeth and Caroline, who could pass for natural mother and daughter. The Frankenstein family called Elizabeth "cousin" instead of sister. In the nineteenth century this term meant a distant relative. First cousins could legally marry so it diffused the incestuous brother/sister context of the pairing.

When a man looks across the room and instantly "falls in love" with a woman, it is the anima part of his Self that sees in the woman a conduit for his anima's projections. Victor's mother has executed this function on his behalf, unconsciously to project her own agenda.

Literary scholars identify the character of Elizabeth as Mary Shelley's fantasy persona. Both were orphaned at birth, but Elizabeth got the "good" stepmother. A man's anima develops with influences from his mother, sisters, and lovers. Elizabeth is Victor's mother-trained, hand-picked, sister and lover-to-be.

I recall as a small boy how wondrous and all-knowing my mother seemed. She instantly knew what I was feeling and put names to disappointments, fears, and happiness. My father scorned my sixth grade choir concert as a sissified waste of time, but my mother was aware I truly enjoyed the event. The projection of a boy's feeling function upon the women continues in his life, as do the drawbacks. When a boy's emotions are not adequately interpreted by his mother, he pouts or throws a tantrum. When an adult man expects a woman to understand his feelings, he is equally disappointed when she does not. An extension of the problem of relegating emotional processing to women is that men come to distrust that other men can understand their feelings.

I was five years old when a new type of feminine experience arrived in my life. It came from nowhere. It was early summer and I was playing in the sandbox with an older female cousin who was sexually attractive. At five I had no clue concerning sexual attraction, but I was fascinated by the appearance of this blonde girl. She excited me in a heretofore unknown sense. I got my first conscious erection, immediately connecting it to female desire. I haven't asked other men if they knew the moment they were heterosexual or gay, but this was my defining moment.

The following dream came to me at age twelve.

> *I am at a camp and there are bunk beds to sleep upon. The most enticing and beautiful girl about my age enters the room and then climbs into my cot. She is French and we do not speak, but I am instantly and totally taken by her beauty and my intense feelings of love and the desire for union with her.*

This dream captures a man's intense desire to experience his anima. I am unable to communicate with the girl in my dream because she speaks French. Actually I am too young at age twelve for the next step of a sexualized projection. My dream anima appears out of nowhere as a female about my same age. She is mysterious and captivating, qualities that signify the anima in a man's dream.

Boys are filled with testosterone-powered aggression and competition which easily distract and overshadow their capacity sit quietly, experience emotions, and do reflection. These feminine-toned functions that are carried by their mothers in childhood are transferred during adolescence to love interests, jumping like sparks from a cut power line as serial crushes on schools girls, movie stars, cheerleaders, and teachers. As a man matures the anima function gets specifically focused and projected onto a specific lover.

Elizabeth's arrival in the Frankenstein house initiates Victor's transfer of the anima projection. Importantly for our discussion is that Victor's mother is the agent of the transfer. She handpicks her successor to carry Victor's anima projection, but because his mother controls his anima, she makes the choice according to her agenda.

My favorite songs that typify anima projection are Roy Orbison's *Pretty Woman* and Lionel Richie's *Hello*. In the former, the singer sees a pretty woman walking down the street and he is immediately swept away with love and desire. In *Hello* the man sings, "I've been alone with you inside my mind," "In my dreams I've kissed your lips a thousand times," "I can see it in your eyes, I can see it in your smile," "You're all I've ever wanted," "Is it me you're looking for?" This is the power of the anima that plummets a man into "a fool in love."

Many men are dumbfounded why they are repeatedly attracted to a certain type of woman, and why that attraction leads to a string of disastrous relationships. A man with this history needs to investigate his mother-complex. Likely he expects the women to whom he is bonding, to carry his anima projection with perfection. He becomes angry at their failure. The women become frustrated and eventually angry or disinterested that they cannot understand or fulfill his emotional needs. Correcting this repetitive pattern of failed relationships requires the man consciously transform his mother-complex and develop an internal relationship with his anima.

Victor's mother arranges his engagement to Elizabeth with the complicity of Victor's father without input from Victor. The old song lyrics say, "I want a girl just like the girl who married dear old dad." Caroline has essentially cloned herself in Elizabeth, but the gift of Caroline is not of Victor's choosing and she is unlikely to satisfy his anima's needs.

One of my best friends from high school always dated women who were very similar to his mother. Physically they were heavy-set with large breasts; personality-wise they had soft demeanors of quiet acceptance. My experience was the opposite of his. I had a delightful and sweet mother, but she lacked the drive and power that my anima required in a prospective projectee. Because my mother was often not up to the task of carrying my demanding emotional needs as a boy, I had many temper outbursts. Later I looked for a new anima carrier who was feisty enough for the task. I can recall my sentiments as a man in my twenties when the urge for marriage became constellated. My male friends and I began discussing potential marriage prospects. We changed our dating habits to a search for Ms. Right. That meant one or two dates with a woman and if there was no future potential as a wife, i.e. she was not a hook for anima projection.

Although I was not attracted to women who were like my mother, did that mean that I was without a mother-complex? I wish. It would have saved me thousands of dollars and hours of therapy years later. We all have mothers who have carried our anima projections and left us with mother-complexes. Although I had some consciousness about wanting a woman unlike my mother, I was a "sucker" for women with a certain look of painful despondency that was like my mother's. Their despondent look, "take care of me," hooked the projection of my own dependency needs.

The history of therapy has too much mother-bashing. This chapter's discussion of mother-complexes is not maligning the actual mothers. The analysand needs to understand that his emotional needs were legitimate, but his mother's inability to modulate them perfectly is inevitable, and his mother-complex exists and is related to his experience with his mother. The same logic applies to his wife or lover; she also is unable to modulate his emotional needs perfectly. His task in therapy is to learn to manage his own emotional life. When a man in therapy has a litany of complaints about his wife and their fighting, it is time to explore his inner feminine that needs his attention. The analysand may want soothing attention from his spouse, but he must discover how to comfort the unhappy anima within.

One source for the tragic outcomes of *Frankenstein* is that Victor never differentiates his inner anima from his mother's agenda. He capitulates to marrying Elizabeth with eventual disaster. The arranged marriage is a parental usurpation of a child's Self. Victor's parents conspired to control his outer life (family assets) and his inner life (Elizabeth = soul/anima). The insightful reader may laugh and ask, "If we choose mates based on our unconscious parental introjects, does it matter if our parents actually arrange our marriages?" Considering that most of the six billion people on the planet have whole or partially arranged marriages with similar issues of divorce, infidelity, and abuse as in non-arranged marriages, it may not seem to matter. However, the freedom to choose one's spouse at least offers some hope for the individuation process to the extent parental introjects are less active. Arranged marriages are enacted for social goals and ignore the psychic goals of the individual.

Elizabeth is the name of a well-known cousin in the Western psyche. She was Mary's cousin who abetted God in caring for Mary during the gestation of Jesus. Elisha, Elijah, and Eliza are derivative names of Jehovah, the Hebrew god. Beth can mean "house of" or "helper." Bethel often refers to a temple or other house of god or the means to assist god. So Elizabeth (god's helper) is a cousin who is abetting the parents (external god-image) in taking over the feminine (Victor's anima).

A child is up against a mountain of parental introjects beyond Mom's preference for the mother of her grandchildren. Religious training is imposed. Social structure and status are imposed. Nationality and cultural duties are imposed. There is little room for individual uniqueness. It's a big mountain.

Some parents fantasize that beating good ideas and morals into their children causes them to live exemplary lives. The plan may seem like a perfect recipe for success; however, from a depth psychology viewpoint, it fails to acknowledge the importance of the unique inner psychic life and agenda of the child. Worse, it fails to understand the potential suffering it can cause from diminution of the Self. Actual arranged marriages are on the decline in the West, but children still fear bringing potential spouses home to meet the parents for approval. In Shelley's 19th century Europe, the practice of arranged marriage had been watered down to parental suggestions.

Parental-complexes are like tapes playing in the back our heads with mother and father singing refrains that begin with "you should." Parental instructions that coincide with our psychic agendas are syncretic, and there is no psychic trauma. But parental introjects that conflict with true desire wound our souls. Disobeying parental introjects causes feelings of guilt and disloyalty. The skilled analyst uses his transference bond to become a surrogate parent to grant the analysand permission to combat parental introjects.

Parental-complexes are allied with the culture to produce shadow contents. A common cultural fear that a boy will not be tough enough induces the parents to introject toughness. Beginning about age six most boys are taught to react without tears or gentle feelings; bravery and courage to enter competition and combat are expected. This pushes a boy's sensitivities into his shadow, and as men approach adulthood their personas respond to cultural pressures with increasing machismo. They may act tough and clever to attract women and assert their presence in the outer world. The ambitious become serious about education and career. Military recruiters proclaim they are, "looking for a few good men." Actually, they are looking for young men with male bravado that the military can exploit.

But some men flee in psychic terror from the functional adult male world. These fly- away-boys, Peter Pans, or "puer eternae" (Latin for eternal boys) shun responsibility and commitment. They cling to home, or become beach bums. They refuse to marry, or if they do, they expect their wives to mother them. They flit from job to job without true ambition. In one sense, the Peter Pan is wise to reject adopting an inauthentic persona. On the other hand, he becomes a cultural monster. His "fly-away" activities create pain for those wanting to sustain a relationship with him. The Peter Pan is a special form of the male monster expressing shadow libido. The cure for the puer eturnus is achieving a consciousness of his individual agenda that causes him to flee. He can then find a balance that preserves his uniqueness while participating usefully and peacefully within the boundaries of society.

NOTES FOR CHAPTER 1:

1. The first item of a man's therapy is to detoxify from abuse or addiction. This is a prerequisite before any depth transformations can occur.

Question: Are there serious issues of trauma or abuse in your life that need special attention?

2. Step two is to grant oneself the permission to change introjects from parents, church, and society as necessary.

Question: Are you open to rejecting the "shoulds" and "musts" you are expected to follow?

3. Third, the analysand adopts a therapeutic framework of his current state of distress: This is where I am; I got here honestly; I don't need to blame anyone; I will not complain; I intend to move forward.

Question: Have you given up blaming your parents and accepted that they have done the best they could, and that you are fully responsible for your emotional life?

NOTES FOR MOTHER-COMPLEX WORK

1. From birth, our mothers have carried our feeling function that organizes our emotions. Our wives likely carry much of this now.

Question: What emotions do you find difficult to process and prefer to relegate to women?

2. We have an introjections (ideas and demands originating from outside us) that came from our mothers and deeply influence the expression and organization of our emotions, i.e., the mother-complex.

Questions: Can you identify times when you pretended to feel or respond a certain way because that was expected of you?

Are there times when you are confused and unable to determine your honest emotions?

Can you separate your desires from those of your mother or wife without guilt or discomfort?

3. Variant expressions of the mother-complex include over-idealization of women, fear of women, anger at women, mistrust, detachment from feelings, over-valuing sexual experience, under-valuing emotional response, etc.

Question: What was your mother's style of emotional responses for you? What mother-related feelings about women from the above list describe you?

4. The goals of mother-complex work include:

A. Separate my mother's feelings from my feelings
B. See my mother/woman partner as separate person
C. Accept the faults and values of women
D. Experience fully my personal emotions, naming them and appropriately responding
E. Develop empathy for others

5. Mother-complex issues are suggested by dreams about angry or judgmental women, arguments and relationship strife, and patterns of emotional restriction.

Question: Do you have angry women in dreams?

6. Moodiness, anger, and irritability, particularly when focused at a woman, are generally signs of a mother-complex issue.

Question: Can you link triggers from arguments with your wife with origins in your childhood?

7. The mother-complex is associated with feeling-toned behaviors:
Questions:

A. What traits of my mother have I adopted?
B. What do I like most about my mother?
C. What do I dislike most about my mother?
D. What induces pain in my mother?
E. What unachieved goals in my mother's life do I carry?
F. How are the women in my life like my mother?

8. What did my mother tell me about my father, "good" and "bad", that sticks in my head?

9. What family curses, patterns of discord or tragedy, are present in my mother's family?

CHAPTER 2

Victor tells Robert Walton he admired Henry's vivaciousness and Elizabeth's tender ability to lighten his mood:

> "My temper was sometimes violent...."

(Ch 2, par 4)

> "The saintly soul of Elizabeth shone like a shrine-dedicated lamp in our peaceful home...She was the living spirit of love to soften and attract: I might have become sullen in my study, rough through the ardour of my nature, but that she was there to subdue me to a semblance of her own gentleness. And Clerval...he might not have been so perfectly humane, so thoughtful in his generosity—so full of kindness and tenderness amidst his passion for adventurous exploit..."

(Ch 2, par 5)

"Rough through the ardour of my nature" aptly conveys Victor's shadow libido. It sours his disposition, erupts as irritability, and is the engine for his compulsions. His psychic organization typifies today's job-focused male: the ego-persona is overworked and the shadow contents are projected. Irritability is a symptom of repressed libido; the soul longs to be doing something else so it festers in agitation. Consider this man's dream early in his therapy:

> *The dreamer descends stairs into the basement. There is a room which he enters and the door closes behind him, revealing it is a prison cell filled with despairing people.*

The prisoners are ignored shadow personalities. His ego is the warden that is exhausting psychic and bodily energy to keep them locked out of consciousness. Science work becomes Victor's compulsion that excludes and imprisons his unexpressed personalities. Moodiness and sullenness are pleas of despondent shadow prisoners. Eventually their pleas will become more vengeful.

Compulsions serve to divert the pleas of the unconscious. They take many forms including excessive work at the office, tinkering about the house, sport fanaticism, political ranting, substance abuse, commuter games, gambling, television watching, eating, and my favorite, golf. I am sadly reminded of my father who exhibited two main compulsions. The first was working around the house. Often he would re-pack wheel bearings on his car or clean a carburetor unnecessarily. His second compulsion was Saturday escapes to a boyhood friend's farm. He sought companionship and spent the day farming. The purpose of his compulsions was to ward off the depressive affect from his suppressed unconscious. Ultimately his compulsions lost the battle to his unconscious and he committed suicide. In the period just before my father's suicide at age forty-six, my mother was bewildered watching him compulsively cleaning the walls of the basement. The metaphor of cleaning the basement is an image of the exhaustive energy required to keep shadow characters from escaping the prison of unconsciousness. The lesson I learned from his death is that avoidance through compulsions ultimately fails.

Three significant hurdles impede depressed patients. First, depressed patients lack self-permission to experience new opportunities. Hopeless patients are convinced their lives can never change. Second, depressed persons often cannot identify their true desires. Acknowledging one's shadow and accepting the validity of its expression requires ego strength. A man with too weak an ego continues to run from the totality of his unconscious. We will see that this is part of Victor's problem. Third, depressed patients have difficulty accessing the courage and energy to pursue their desires once identified.

Victor has an inkling that his true desire is to study alchemy. He lacks permission via his father-complex to pursue the studies when his father pooh-poohs his interest:

> **"Ah! Cornelius Agrippa!** (Victor's favorite alchemist.) **My dear Victor, do not waste your time upon this; it is sad trash..."**
>
> **(Chap 2, par 7)**

The alchemists' opus was the transformation of base metals, the prima materia, into gold. Carl Jung identified that alchemy was a metaphor for an unconscious ritual of psychic transformation. "Making gold" to a Jungian psychologist means individuation, developing reverence for the Self and engaging the ego into service of its authentic wholeness.

> **"I entered with the greatest diligence into the search of the philosopher's stone and the elixir of life; but the latter soon attained my undivided attention."**
>
> **(Chap 2, par 11)**

Unknowingly alchemists conflated physical and psychological elements in their work. Like them, Victor has no idea what he is doing psychologically. He confuses elixir of life, i.e. science of life, with the life of his soul. But he has a true to desire to learn more about alchemy because his soul knows that the pursuit of alchemical studies has a nurturing quality. Victor's ego believes he is pursuing a noble mission to decipher the science of conquering death, but his unconscious is pursuing wholeness.

The Self has a scanning function that pursues its desire for individuation. It draws Victor to the alchemical aspects of self-reflection. For an intelligent man like Victor, a foray into the reflection on the personal meaning of life is what he needs. Although Victor's Self attracts him to alchemy, his ego capitulates to his father's rejection of philosophy, thus driving it into Victor's shadow.

My father denigrated studying literature and the arts. I once considered becoming a journalist. I read voraciously, arising at 4 a.m. to read several hours before the school bus arrived. My father considered literature and writing to be a waste of time. I accepted that these activities would need to be done in secret, while my father slept.

Like Victor I enjoyed the sciences and became a physician. By age thirty-five I was suffering the consequences of too little attention to my creative needs. I felt empty and anxious to do something. Had I fully rejected my soul's calling for balance, I might have become a suicide statistic also.

My unconscious desire to write was expressed outwardly as contempt for authors whom I found mediocre. They were not, in my opinion, worthy of their fame: my expression of classical sour-grapes. If what we desire appears unobtainable or is forbidden, it is commonly treated with contempt. Fire-and-brimstone preachers fit in here. I expressed my contempt with cutting sarcasm and insults.

Fortunately I have a wife who intuited my problem. Most men benefit from the assistance of women at special times in their lives. If men had more contact with their intuition, they would need less female assistance in identifying and pursuing cut-off needs. My wife signed me up for a mystery writing class and persuaded me to attend. My first effort was an awful mystery that I wrote as a stage play. Within weeks I began to withdraw my sour-grapes criticism of writing and to realize I yearned to be a playwright, not a mystery writer. My own writing brought me to appreciate the efforts of other writers, especially the complexity of the great playwrights. I felt my shadow writer converting its expression from contempt to appreciation. As I write this book I continue to write plays, an activity that gives me purpose and joy.

Victor continues reading alchemy but on the sly; adolescents do rebel against having their souls co-opted. I was a teen in the sixties when adolescents revolted against a stifling American culture by turning to free love and drugs. Today's teenagers rebel by wearing outrageous clothes, committing vandalism, and playing counter-culture obscene rap music. Teens "act out" because they lack the consciousness to maturely balance their inner soul needs against the constrictions of the culture.

Victor's father-complex wins the battle when Victor pushes it into his shadow prison:

"All that had so long engaged my attention suddenly grew despicable."

(Chap 2, par 14)

The therapeutic challenge of helping men identify their desires is difficult. A man will say, "I don't know what I want," but often can express what he doesn't like, such as "I don't want to go to work any more." If asked what is offensive or lacking at work, he may respond, "It's boring." This likely means that creative experience is what the analysand craves.

Victor is synchronistically warned about abandoning alchemy during a violent thunderstorm when a lightning bolt strikes and explodes a tree. Victor witnesses the burning stump of what was previously a beautiful oak tree, a metaphor for the life of his Self. In dreams, as in art, storms symbolize flooding from the unconscious. The storm arose rapidly over the top of Jura, the Swiss equivalent of Olympus, a metaphor of retribution from angry gods. This is a pivotal moment for Victor: whether to become reverent to the gods of personal transformation, or to cast aside humility and aspire to be a godlike through his subsequent monster creation. The lightning bolt to the tree and later a flash illuminating the monster at night are the only incidences of lightning in the novel, but screenwriters have highlighted lightning as the force that animates the monster in Frankenstein's laboratory.

The burning stump metaphor for Victor's Self (tree of life) echoes the Promethean theme of Frankenstein as a reference to Zeus, the thunderbolt god, revenging Prometheus' for stealing fire. The oak tree is a symbol of Zeus. When Victor creates life from death, he is stealing power from the gods externally, from his Self internally. The burning stump is an omen that Victor's ego will receive revenge from the Self.

Victor's monster development accelerates as he begins experimenting to revive the dead. Victor describes to Walton the moment he committed himself to the pursuit of science in lieu of his other inclinations.

> **"Thus strangely are our souls constructed, and by such slight ligaments are we bound to prosperity or ruin. When I look back, it seems to me as if this almost miraculous change of inclination and will was the immediate suggestion of the guardian angel of my life—the last effort made by the spirit of preservation to avert the storm that was even then hanging in the stars, and ready to envelope me. Her** [he is referring to the angel of destiny] **victory was announced by an unusual tranquility and gladness of soul, which followed the relinquishing of my ancient and latterly tormenting studies. It was thus that I was to be taught to associate evil with their prosecution, happiness with their disregard."**
>
> **(Chap 2, par 15)**

Victor's monster transformation congeals as his ego decides that attending to his soul's desire of alchemical reflection has become evil. Once authentic desire is shut out, the forces of vengeance are consolidated.

We witness this consolidation in terrorist suicide bombings. Repressed desires such as sexual gratification, material goods, or personal freedoms get projected onto another country. The pent-up libido of unexpressed desire is now available for malicious acts. Anticipatory delight of a reward in the afterlife sustains the ego's denial and repression of shadow libido. Fundamentalist Christians, who welcome the apocalypse, have vengeful shadows of sexuality, feminine equality, and independent thinking. Some delight in anticipating the death and suffering of non-believers. Rapture is the Christian ego's reward for enduring the pains of repression. Rapist-murderers, denied their feeling functions and sexuality, derive pleasure from ritual sexual mutilation.

The *Frankenstein* tale warns that rejected monsters enact revenge. In psychological terms, shadow rejection implies placing the ego above the totality of the Self. A repressed Self creates anger that may lead to vengeance. Psychologically repressing the Self is the religious equivalent of the loss of the soul and a life in hell.

At first glance this business of acquiescing to Victor's father may seem trivial. What could be the harm of not reading alchemy? A boy's psychic organization projects his immature Self onto his father. A man receives his structural program of manhood from his father. This means that the boy inculcates his father's sense of manliness: how to talk like a man, how to act like a man, and how to relate to women. He internalizes his father's judgment of what constitutes duty and honor. Most boys mimic the actions of their fathers. Other boys, however, develop strong negative-father complexes and reject the ways of their fathers. Regardless, a boy's manliness is modulated through his father-complex: either be like dad or be the opposite of dad. Consequently a boy reaches adulthood with a long list of inner rules dictating behavior and acceptability. The psychologist Alfred Adler would call the ideas, "fictions," personal made up rules and beliefs that determine behavior.

For example, I suffered (until helped through analysis) from a sense of shame as a man because I wore a tie. Deep in my psyche, the image of a real man was like my factory-worker father, a laborer who got dirty and wore work clothes. To this day I watch painters, plumbers, and carpenters with awe. These are real men to my psyche. Until I discovered this aspect of my indoctrinated manhood, I felt shame and was apologetic of my professional career.

Many mothers complain that their teenage sons treat them disrespectfully like their fathers do. These sons have internalized the behaviors of their fathers as father-complex scripts to belittle, ignore, and insult women including their mothers.

Extreme cases of father-complex control of behavior are family curses. These commonly include the addictions of smoking and alcoholism. The son has an internal program that says: to be a real man and to honor the father that I love, I must be like him and smoke or drink. The success of the Marlboro Man ads lies in its ability to instill the image of the real man smoking Marlboro brand cigarettes. Family curses are explored more deeply in chapter seven.

NOTES FOR CHAPTER 2

1. The ego actively suppresses the aspects of the Self that it finds unacceptable. The rejected parts of the Self become assembled within the shadow as a libidinous entity, the monster.

Questions: What actions do you find intolerable in others?

Can you fantasize yourself performing those actions?

2. Immense energy and time are consumed in repressing the inner monster. Often this manifests in compulsive activities.

Questions: What are your compulsive activities?

What emotions are prohibited or avoided during your compulsions?

CHAPTER 3

The first family tragedy strikes when Victor is seventeen. Elizabeth is stricken with scarlet fever, a potentially lethal streptococcal infection in the pre-antibiotic era. Elizabeth, Victor's emerging anima figure, is febrile with a red rash from sepsis. Hot and uncomfortable is an apt image for the emotional state of an adolescent boy. Will Victor's feminine survive?

Victor's mother nurses Elizabeth, her "favorite child," through the precarious illness back to health. The tragedy is that Victor's mother contracts the infection and dies. A psychological metaphor for the death of his mother and survival of Elizabeth is that Victor has replaced his mother as his primary anima carrier and transferred his anima projection to a woman his own age.

Victor's mother remains perfectly graceful and loving even on her deathbed. Without complaint, she expresses only the best wishes for her family.

> **"My children," she said, "My firmest hopes of future happiness were placed on the prospect of your union…. Alas! I regret that I am taken from you; and, happy and beloved as I have been, is it not hard to quit** (archaic, meaning: leave) **you all? But these are not thoughts befitting me; I will endeavor to resign myself cheerfully to**

71

death, and will indulge a hope of meeting you in another world."

(Chap 3, par 2)

Elizabeth is now separated from her stepmother at age seventeen, the age when Mary Wollstonecraft ran away from her stepmother with Percy Shelley. Mary Shelley demonstrates that whether we have natural or stepparents, our psyches construct images of ideal parents. Parental idealization is a great hurdle in overcoming parental complexes because our psychic software instructs us not to disappoint a good parent. The good inner father must not be betrayed. Victor has two parental idealizations to overcome.

Tribal initiations succeed in separating boys from their mothers, but do not eradicate their mother-complexes. Severing a boy's relationship with his mother causes grief that is symbolized by Victor Frankenstein's grief for his dead mother. Separating a boy from his mother dissolves his enmeshment with her and diminishes her access for his anima modulation. Typically boys take on an insensitive machismo attitude, but his immature anima is unchanged and must go somewhere. The anima gets packed into a psychological holding cell. The anima becomes the metaphoric maiden in the castle who is held hostage by a dragon. The dragon represents the male ego's grandiose persona that imprisons his anima in the castle dungeon.

The mother-complex creates a split duality. The good/nurturing mother is often imaged as one's fairy godmother. The wicked witch is a metaphor of the bad/devouring aspects of the mother. Examples include the child-eating witch in Hansel and Gretel and the narcissistic stepmother of Cinderella. The bad mother is the personification of life's harsh realities. Hardship, sickness, disappointment, and death are inevitable. As much as we wish to avoid or conquer these dark aspects of Mother Nature, ultimately, we must suffer and die. Psychological health necessitates a truce with the witch and an acceptance of life's cruelty to allow us to experience life's emotional richness and to feel meaning. Seventeen-year-old Victor splits his feminine projections of good (mother and Elizabeth) from bad (forces of death that have taken his mother's life).

Today's teenage boy gets little cultural assistance separating from his mother. His attempts often manifest as silly swaggering, dressing in baggy clothes, or exhibiting a bravado persona of the current counter-culture. The beatniks of the fifties, the hippies of the sixties, the grungies of the eighties, and the rapsters and goths of recent decades are adolescent attempts at psychological independence from parents and culture. One reason that the presence of his father is valuable to an adolescent boy is to buffer the separation from mother, providing a grounded example of maintaining a relationship with the boy's mother that has appropriate boundaries.

Grieving in the days after his mother's funeral, Victor delays his departure for university. He clings to the companionship and healing presence of his friend, Henry Clerval, who assists Victor to process his grief. Victor in turn encourages Henry's wish to travel to Ingolstadt, Germany, and attend university with Victor. The healthiest and most hopeful moments of *Frankenstein* occur when Victor and Henry interact. They balance each other and increase one another's joy. Their relationship is a metaphor for the joy that results from accessing one's least expressed psychic part, the inferior function.

Mr. Clerval, Henry's father, considers school for learning's sake a foolish waste of time. Victor departs for Ingolstadt University, but Henry's father demands Henry stay home to learn the business trade of the family and prepare himself to earn a living. Victor is distressed to leave his friend, but patriarchal forces part them.

> **"We could not tear ourselves away from each other, nor persuade ourselves to say the word, "Farewell!"**
>
> (Chap 3, par 7)

Victor obsesses over Elizabeth's grieving for their mother. A mature Victor would feel empathy for Elizabeth's grief as a sister and independent person. But because she holds Victor's anima, her grieving is also the pain of his suppressed anima, hence his obsessive over-reaction.

His mother is dead, he is separated from Henry, and his anima carrier is crying in pain: Victor has hit an emotional trifecta of grief. He leaves for school to lessen his pain. In true male form, he dumps his emotional work onto his anima carrier as a safety valve to protect himself against a flood of emotional craziness, then heads for the nearest exit. The younger the man, the more difficult and painful it is to sustain emotional discomfort. Victor's ego is not large enough to hold his grief and feel empathy for Elizabeth simultaneously; ergo, he flees.

The exit doors of emotional avoidance include denial, projection, and distraction. Work, hobbies, sports, or couch-potato TV viewing are often pursued more to protect against emotional flooding than for the intrinsic joy of the activities.

Modulating emotions is the role of the feeling function. It has a wavy and watery aspect like the sea. The feminine dominant psyche of women is naturally better at sustaining the tides of emotions. In contrast the anima/feminine function in a man is neither dominant nor conscious, thus strong emotions flood him with fright and discomfort. The inability to sustain and modulate emotions causes men to become moody, or to clam up, or respond physically inappropriately. Women misinterpret a man's inability to converse about his emotional state as withdrawing or distancing when he is simply incapable of maintaining an ego consciousness in the presence of strong emotions.

The more immature the anima connection of a man, the more likely he will respond to strong emotions with rage. Many domestic arguments erupt over seemingly trivial items such as scheduling activities or doing household projects. What often follows from a wife's innocent request, "Honey, would you mow the grass today?" is that her husband becomes flooded with negative feelings: disapproval from his wife, inadequacy as a husband, disappointment at not having time to play golf, and irritation at his wife for usurping his free time. The man with an immature anima connection cannot hold multiple feelings. His container is too weak. He may pout, become angry, or storm out of the house. Learning to contain emotions is assisted by having a mentor who can model sustaining strong emotions without craziness. Being near a woman with a mature feeling function does little to help an immature man because he will attempt to have her do his emotional work for him.

At Ingolstadt University, Victor is introduced to two contrasting mentors. The first is a grumpy but intelligent science instructor, Professor Krempe. His name connotes to crimp, to stifle or to fold. In German, the word "krempe" means bedeviling or teasing. Victor's life is being bent in a dangerous direction as he follows the advice of Professor Krempe. A crimp is also a man who uses trickery to conscript boys into serving on naval ships. Shelley has a subtle parallel to Robert Walton's crimping seduction of his sailing crew, promising them fame if they discover a northwest passage, but discounting the danger to them.

Echoing Victor's father, Professor Krempe rebukes Victor for wasting his thoughts on alchemy. The professor hands Victor a substitute reading list geared to serious modern science studies. Victor doesn't like Krempe but respects him and aspires to acquire his knowledge. Thus Krempe assumes an in-loco-parentis role perpetuating Victor's father-complex.

Victor is also mentored by a chemistry professor named Waldman, who is gentler and wiser than Krempe. Waldman's German name means "world man," one with a perspective of totality. Unlike Krempe who "crimps" Victor's desire to study alchemy, Professor Waldman values philosophy and the soul work of the alchemists, although he favors rigorous science.

> **"The ancient teachers of this science promised impossibilities, and performed nothing. The modern masters promise very little; they know that metals cannot be transmuted, and that the elixir of life is a chimera. But these philosophers, whose hands seem only made to dabble in dirt; and their eyes to pore over the microscope or crucible, have indeed performed miracles. They penetrate into the recesses of nature, and show how she works in her hiding places. They ascend into the heavens; they have discovered how the blood circulates, and the nature of the air we breathe. They have acquired new and almost unlimited powers; they can command the thunders of heaven, mimic the earthquake, and even mock the invisible world with its own shadows."**
>
> **(Chap 3, par 14)**

Victor hears only the professor's words that encourage him to delve deeper into science. What Victor does not hear is Professor Waldman's suggestion he not restrict his studies exclusively to science,

> **"A man would make but a very sorry chemist if he attended to that department of human knowledge alone."**
>
> **(Chap 3, par 17)**

Victor develops an obsession for studying science that disrupts the balance in his life by shutting off his social needs. For two years he does not return home to visit and rarely writes. Work without play makes one more than dull; it stokes an inner monster.

NOTES FOR CHAPTER 3

1. The anima function of feeling modulation and expression is immature in a boy. Initially it is carried by the mother. From adolescent development through later life a man seeks women closer to his age for transfer of his anima projection.

Question: What is most attractive or important trait to you in a woman?

2. Young men often cannot sustain strong emotions that flood their ability to be present. A man cannot articulate his emotional states when he has been overtaken by a "mood." Often a young man flees from emotional experience, or he acts out in rage.

Question: How do you typically respond to stressful emotions? Do you leave, become a detached problem solver, get angry, or become quietly clam up?

3. The best modulator for a young man learning to process emotions is an older male mentor in whose presence the young man can feel secure, manly, and understood.

Question: Is there a man you admire who expresses authentic emotions in a self-controlled manner?

CHAPTER 4

"Unless I had been animated by an almost supernatural enthusiasm, my application to this study would have been irksome, and almost intolerable. To examine the causes of life, we must first have recourse to death. I became acquainted with the science of anatomy: but this was not sufficient; I must also observe the natural decay and corruption of the human body. In my education my father had taken the greatest precautions that my mind should be impressed with no supernatural horrors. I do not ever remember to have trembled at a tale of superstition, or to have feared the apparition of a spirit. Darkness had no effect upon my fancy; and a churchyard was to me merely a receptacle of bodies deprived of life which, from being the seat of beauty and strength had become food for the worm."

(Chap 4, par 3).

This passage references two forces for monster making. One is the ego's identification with divine power, i.e., ego identification with the power of the Self. Victor's ego has a grandiose god-like feeling of self-importance to conquer death with a sense of invincibility and unaccountability. The second force of monster making is

Victor's fearless scoffing at the supernatural. From the intra-psychic perspective this means discounting the divine spiritual life of the "other world." The divine "other world" to the ego is the Self. To dismiss the spirit world is to reject the needs of the Self.

Victor says he has "supernatural enthusiasm," aligning himself with the gods of creation. Enthusiasm is redundant, when pared with supernatural, as it means filled (en) with divine spirit (theos). The danger of excessive enthusiasm is that humans have a limited capacity to sustain godliness. The story of Icarus mentioned earlier tells of the peril to humans who get too close to archetypal super-human energies. Victor is doubling down on his perilous luck when he exalts his grandiose ego and shuns reverence for his spiritual Self.

Victor's obsession with his science studies typifies the professional obsession of many accountants, doctors, lawyers, and MBA's who lose their sense of humor and become intensely serious and focused. They neglect family and friends. The distance from their souls can be seen in their faces as a lack of animation. A friend's son who is naturally gregarious with numerous friends, obtained an MBA degree and pursued Wall Street banking. His face has become serious and sad; his demeanor, stressed and lifeless. He is like Victor: absorbed with the powers of creation (money in his case, science in Victor's), and disconnected from his soul. Movies and novels abound with male characters that are emotionally stifled by their ambitions. "Mr. Banks," the father and banker in *Mary Poppins,* and Scrooge in *A Christmas Carol* are examples.

As ambition draws men away from the balancing aspects of their lives, libido associated with the left-behind parts of our personality moves to the shadow. The greater the separation and the longer the interval that a man is distanced from his lesser functions, the greater the potential for that libido to surface as an angry monster.

Self-esteem is healthy when it honestly reflects a man's talent, providing courage to function in the world. Pathologic grandiosity is a god-like sense of brilliance and invulnerability. In fairy tales it is represented by the dragon who keeps an imprisoned damsel whom the mythic hero must rescue. Psychologically the dragon that must be slain is the ego's attitude of control. The damsel is the anima (emotional flow and feeling function of a man) who once freed has the opportunity to mature into a queen. Becoming a queen and sharing rule of the psychic kingdom with the masculine is an image of individuation.

Victor's study of death is an ego-guided battle to preserve his mother-complex, not a Self-initiated transformation. His unconscious motivation for conquering death is to revive his lost anima that his mother carried. Although his mother assigned his anima to Elizabeth, the transfer was incomplete. His resistance in transferring his anima energy from his mother to Elizabeth is symbolized in Victor's inability to commit to a wedding date with her.

Although Victor is trying to overcome his fear of death in a socially acceptable way, he invites trouble when he attempts to conquer death. Paradoxically, to experience fullness in life one must develop an acceptance of death. Death can be a positive metaphor used to assist transformation. The archetype of resurrection conveys that death of one life-stage ends and a new stage is born. In tribal initiations elders deliver a scar, circumcision, or tooth extraction to depict death of a boy's attachment to his mother and the birth of his manhood.

Gaining knowledge of death, the dead, and the meaning of death is a recurring theme in many epic stories. Odysseus, Jesus, and Faust are heroes who visit the underworld of the dead in order to renew their lives. A man's journey to the land of the dead teaches him that he cannot redeem his ancestors. Relatives are a connection via bloodline, but their lives are distinct and separate. The members of one's tribe, church, or race are also separate human beings. Psychologically, leaving the underworld and returning to the land of the living means that a man leaves the complexes of his ancestors and becomes responsible to his Self. He must forego trying to live out a cultural expectation, a religious prescription, or a similar ancestral doctrine in lieu of an authentic life.

Victor Frankenstein's pursuit of reviving the dead contravenes the cycle of accepting death and moving on to the next stage of life. Perhaps if he had pursed his alchemical studies and learned of alchemical "mortification," the processing cycle of death and re-birth, he could have accepted the pain of his mother's passing.

Traditional religions have taboos against directly accessing the gods. Only the shamans and spiritual leaders who have been trained in the dangers of grandiose inflation are allowed to confront the divine powers. Victor is not alone in his god-like inflation. The television gives witness to slam-dunking athletes, television evangelists, shouting pundits, and war-promoting politicos.

Psychologist Carl Jung remarked that the problem of modernity is that man no longer has a mythic buffer of protection from archetypal and spiritual forces. Traditional religions have lost the power of divine containment for many people to the anger of fundamentalists. For those for whom religion is meaningless, the task is to discover and/or create a new myth for spiritual modulation. In other words, modern man is in search of a new god-image to buffer him against the psychosis of becoming possessed with too much divine energy. Victor has no container for his ascent to the realm of the creation gods, as he plunges ahead.

> **"The astonishment which I had at first experienced on this discovery soon gave place to delight and rapture."**
>
> **(Chap 4, par 5)**

Rapture is a state of ecstasy. The secular meaning of rapture has been replaced by a specific Christian evangelical reference: ascent to heaven as a reward to the righteous at the onset of Armageddon. Christian fundamentalists eagerly await an impending apocalypse. They have identified with God through their righteousness. This inflated identification with God is similar to Victor's feeling from discovering the secrets for re-animating the dead. The ego experiences a god-identified state as rapture because nothing feels greater than being equal to God.

There is a sinister side to the fundamentalists' wish for the apocalypse. The monster parts of their psyches wish vengeance and death to those who have experienced life's totality, i.e. the non-righteous who have accepted and integrated "sin" that has been denied to them by religious dogma. There is a sinister delight in anticipating death and torture to those outside the religious tribe. War and genocide are sadistic pleasures for the righteous. When the U.S. began bombing Iraq in 2003, I was in an airport as the invasion was broadcast on television. People in the waiting area cheered and gloated at each explosion. I felt I was at the Roman Circus witnessing lions eating Christians. Similarly when the World Trade Center was destroyed, Muslim sympathizers celebrated in the streets of Palestine. The enjoyment of killing innocents is a symptom of monsterism.

The gestation of Victor's monster is quickening as Victor reaches the height of his inflated creative genius. The prologue to the monster's creation is complete. Shelley has given us the list of ingredients for Victor's monster recipe: Victor's mother is dead and his anima is hidden; his father has introjected his parental agenda for Victor's life; Henry and the libido he carries is unavailable; Victor's personal life is unbalanced by his laboratory compulsion; and cultural expectations have separated Victor from his natural desires. His ego-inflation is rampant and has pushed his Self's patience to the limit. The monster in his psychic womb is ready for parturition just as the laboratory monster is about to awaken.

Victor exhibits peculiar symptoms as his monster gets closer to animation. He displays annoyance, irritability, and depression. Victor's sense of becoming "irksome" implies that the pressure from his Self is mounting. His joylessness and depression are symptoms of neglecting his split-off aspects. A person cannot think or work oneself into joy; an overactive ego invites misery. Victor has assembled his wings of wax and is ascending towards the sun:

> "No one can conceive the variety of feelings which bore me onwards, like a hurricane, in the first enthusiasm of success. Life and death appeared to me ideal bounds, which I should first break through, and pour a torrent of light into our dark world. A new species would bless me as its creator and source; many happy and excellent natures would owe his being to me. No father could claim the gratitude of his child so completely as I should deserve theirs."
>
> (Chap 4, par 8)

Victor's identification with God is complete. He envisions himself the creator of a race of grateful beings. Worse, his hubris envisions him being worshipped. The desire to be worshipped is the narcissistic dark side of God. The realm of creating a new species is the province of the collective god image. Victor cannot fulfill his grandiose expectations, but he is determined to give it a go. Dreams of falling, crashing, and public humiliation come to us when our hubris requires deflation. Dreams of being exposed such as being naked in public are expressions of an overly grandiose ego.

The monster's awakening is imminent and Victor is nearly psychotic in his creative frenzy. He is pale and sickly, but he works unceasingly to procure body parts for assembly. Victor becomes drained and nearly delirious. Flowers bloom outside in summer but he cannot take in their pleasure. He is compulsively involved in completing the monster.

> **"I seemed to have lost all soul or sensation but for this one pursuit."**
>
> **(Chap 4, par 9)**

> **"The summer months passed while I was thus engaged, heart and soul, in one pursuit. It was a most beautiful season...but my eyes were insensible to the charms of nature...And the same feelings which made me neglect the scenes around me caused me also to forget those friends who were so many miles absent."**
>
> **(Chap 4, par 10)**

Possession by an archetype will exclude the fullness of life and may destroy one's body. Workaholics are prone to near psychosis, refusing to sleep as they work through the night. They cannot stop working which precludes balancing life activities and relationships. Human beings cannot sustain the unbounded energy investment required in executing an archetypal agenda. Shelley describes Victor's physical body beginning to take on the characteristics of the corpses which he is dissecting and reassembling.

> **"My enthusiasm was checked by my anxiety, and I appeared rather like one doomed by slavery to toil in the mines, or any other unwholesome trade, than an artist occupied by his favourite employment. Every night I was oppressed by a slow fever, and I became nervous to a most**

painful degree; the fall of a leaf startled me, and I shunned my fellow-creatures as if I had been guilty of a crime. Sometimes I grew alarmed at the wreck I perceived that I had become; the energy of my purpose alone sustained me: my labours would soon end...

(Chap 4, par 14)

Victor becomes increasingly ill during his manic monster creation. His edgy vigilance is reminiscent of a cocaine addict. Many men become slaves to their careers only to develop ulcers or heart attacks. Part of every man's soul is lost to "success." Each piece of soul lost increases his propensity toward violence, depression, alcoholism, or anger. Note Victor's word, "unwholesome." Pursuing goals to the exclusion of the whole of the psyche is un-whole, a splitting of the soul.

Victor's father and family write to beg him to return home to visit. He considers the request but decides his work is too important. Victor justifies this for Walton,

"...If no man allowed any pursuit whatsoever to interfere with the tranquility of his domestic affections, Greece had not been enslaved; Caesar would have spared his country; America would have been discovered more gradually; and the empires of Mexico and Peru had not been destroyed."

(Chap 4, par 12)

Victor's implies that these events are good and desirable: the plundering empire of Caesar, Grecian slavery, and the cultural genocides of Peru and Mexico, but are they? These examples are murders committed by men whose god-like hubris was disconnected from their humanity. Perhaps the gravest example is the Third Reich's attempt to exalt the German race.

Dedicated to exalting his ego, Victor makes a Faustian bargain with his shadow parts to catch up on life when the monster is completed:

"I believed that exercise and amusement would then drive

away incipient disease; and I promised myself both of these when my creation should be complete."

(Chap 4, par 14)

How trite is a workaholic's claim that his family is the most important thing to him? Too preoccupied making money to spend time with their families, to vacation, or to attend family outings, they promise themselves that someday they will take it easy. This lie, no matter how well intentioned, belies a slow erosion and eventual soul death for these men. Actions speak louder than words.

NOTES FOR CHAPTER 4

1. The monster is the assembly of split-off needs that are imprisoned in our unconscious. The prison warden is the ego.

Question: Can you name two areas of desire that you do not grant yourself permission to pursue?

2. We develop habits and compulsions to diffuse the pent-up energy of the rejected parts of our psyches.

What are your favorite activities that keep the lesser parts of your Self at bay? Examples: work, alcohol, sports, organizations, or hobbies.

3. The grandiosity of the ego manifests in control over the Self. This grandiosity is a god-like identification.

Question: At what times to you feel especially powerful, clever, or important?

4. Submitting to the agenda of the Self entails a reverent attitude for one's entire being. One must commit his ego to serve his totality (Self). Humility of the ego must be accomplished.

Question: Do you believe in a greater part of you (the Self) that requires your ego's submission?

5. The collective shadow functions in a parallel manner to the individual shadow. It manifests as moral righteousness projecting evil, genocidal atrocities such as those of the Third Reich, colonialism, and imperial warfare.

Question: Whom do you oppress either directly or indirectly, through work or politics: women, children, subordinates, minorities, poor, laborers, or foreigners?

6. Religion has traditionally served as a container against grandiose inflation, both for the individual and society. For many men social and technological evolution has rendered the traditional religions inadequate to contain collective grandiosity. Individual and collective cultures need a new spiritual buffer against inflation.

Questions: What is your spiritual orientation?

Do you have a reverent god-image that is superior to your ego?

CHAPTER 5

Victor's laboratory monster comes to life in one short paragraph that ends with:

"I saw the dull yellow eye of the creature open; it breathed hard, and a convulsive motion agitated its limbs."

(Chap 5, par 1)

Hollywood renditions of the awakening monster include sparking electrodes, bolts through the neck, zigzag scars, and lightning flashes above the observatory roof. Shelley's simple creation scene is one sentence in which the creature opens an eye and breathes. Similarly, our inner monsters are born with little fanfare. But the cognizance of one's shadow is often abrupt, like stepping through a doorway into new building. The prelude to the monster's awakening consumes one-fourth of the *Frankenstein* text. Our monsters take at least one-fourth of our lives before they full develop their autonomous adult personality pattern. Our temper tantrums and outbursts in childhood are like intra-uterine kicking during the gestation of our adult monster.

As a reservoir for shadow libido, the monster is a salubrious construction of the psyche. Society needs prisons to contain its misfits until they are rehabilitated. The psyche needs the shadow to hold libido until it can be usefully integrated. The following dream and subsequent active imagination with the dream figure illustrates holding shadow contents. The analysand (me) experienced this recurring nightmare from age two until age five.

> I am a two-year-old alone on a deserted city street. There is a brick wall behind me. At the base of the wall is a descending stairwell that disappears into the basement level of an unknown building. I am terrified of the basement. More terrifying is the appearance of an adult male wearing a trench coat and a broad brimmed hat. The trench coat man looks about but does not make eye contact with me. Afraid of being harmed by the trench coat man, I brace myself against the brick wall and hope the trench coat man will not notice me. The man looks about again and then descends the stairwell to disappear.

The trench coat man (TCM) lurking in the basement is my shadow. The basement is my unconscious. I fear the shadow man and refuse to engage him. This dream demonstrates that the developing shadow can be present as early as age two. Developmentally it makes sense that this is the period when the shadow is initiated. A two-year-old lacks the ego strength and organization to engage it. The "terrible two's" is the time when a child struggles with rules and order and must relinquish some of his instinctual desires. The child learns he cannot display desires that conflict with his parent's expectations; thus, he pushes these unacceptable desires into his unconscious, to be carried by a shadow being.

Because this dream still contained frightful energy, my therapist insisted that I draw the character and engage it in active imagination. The therapist understood the shadow implications and my need to explore the basement. This is the material I brought to the next session:

As a young child I was too terrified to speak with the trench coat man. But as an adult man of forty I could experience and understand the transformation. In the drawing, the man invites me into the basement. This is the dialogue with the trench coat man:

D (Dreamer):   Mr. Trench Coat Man, I have been so afraid of you. Now I can see that you are trying to escape from a closed room.

T (Trench Coat Man):   Help me.

D: Do you feel like a prisoner?

T: A lonely soul. Suffocating in this room. I am desperate.

D: What room?

T: The shell of forever since your dreams at two.

D: You always terrified me. I thought you would kill me. I hid by leaning into that brick wall.

T: All I did was walk by and look your way. I did see you, but you never knew.
(Although the TCM did not actually speak to me as a child, the picture communicates an invitation to the basement. This is a transformation from memory to the present state of my psyche.)

D: My heart pounds in terror even this minute. Who are you?

T: The power of the left-behind.

D: What do you mean?

T: Years of locking me up in this room.

D: I don't think I can stand this chest pain!

T: How about me?

D: You are talking like the victim here. I am confused. I'm the one who is suffering.

T: We are one, but split; I feel the pain as do you.

D: What do you represent or how can I/we get through this and move forward?

T: I don't know for sure. Let me out! Take off my coat!

D: Does that have a double meaning of mystery and intrigue? How close are you to the inner Self?

T: One part only.

D: Have I been running my life around you? Since age two?

T: You have been avoiding and punishing me.
(This is the way we treat our shadow contents.)

D: I'm sorry. I was a kid. What do you represent? My aggression? My shame? I think the intensity of what I feel is a matrix effect deep down which will cause grief, pain, and a total reorganization of myself if I get into you. I know I must, but it is so painful and I don't know why.

T: I am him, the spirit. Without my coat I stand naked, a man.

D: Him? Him in me? What him?

T: Our mystery. Notice the power and vulnerability of nakedness.

D: All this time I thought you were my father-complex or something.

T: The journey must be made one step at a time. You may have perceived me as evil, but I could have easily been a friend to help you. Think back into the dreams. Walking alone, you just believed the world to be cruel and dangerous. Imagine me helping you find safety.

D: What about the descending stairs?

T: The trip below is always scary. Walk down there now!

D: OK, there are eight steps. I am afraid. Somehow I am a two-year-old right now, not an adult.

T: What do you see inside the basement?

D: Lights and darkness. Warmth, fires, danger, friendly people. I am welcomed. Is this my home? In the underworld?

T: It is a place where you are comfortable and welcomed.

D: Why? Why did I have this dream, this terror? And why has it been so long a time to capture you?

T: It was your story.

D: Have you tried to surface before now?

T: Does not matter.

D: If you are my spirit, do you mean my divine spirit?

T: Awareness of the spirit. See now how your energies have avoided me. The process of seeing demons where none travel.

D: I am sorry to have misjudged you. Also how did I survive without contacting my spirit?

T: You know the answer to that.

D: Oh, alive in the unconscious. I'm having an acute case of "am I making this all up?"

T: You aren't making up the stomach pain and the heart beating.

D: True, but are you sure you aren't my aggression projected? I did think you were evil and terrifying.

T: Think of the coat. It is a mystery. You don't know what is inside. It's a useful way to view the world. It was terrifying for you. The mystery is to find the good in the realm of terror. You came back.

G: Where do we go from here?

T: Wherever we need to. Done for now.

This is a powerful and insightful active imagination. It is considered "active" because the analysand is awake and respectfully interacts with the dream character. Respectful means that the analysand listens and does not bully him. At the same time the analysand can confront the dream character with questions and refuse a request from the dream character if it is judged unacceptable. In order to do active imagination most of us who use writing require a quiet dark room without interruptions.

Several highlights are worthy of comment. I question whether I am "making it up." This is a universal experience of the ego. The ego has difficulty releasing control to the Self (the other within). To maintain control the ego devalues the reality of the imaginal experience. Further, if the ego judges the active imagination content to be foolish fantasy, then the ego is not required to act on its information. Notice that TCM points out that he is not making up the pounding heart and stomach cramps. This is real and terrifying to the ego. The Jungian analyst, Robert Johnson, in an interview said he was told by his therapist, Barbara Hanna, "Yes, your knees will shake and your chest will be squeezed. That's good! It means you are doing it right."

Another common experience is confusion as the dialogue is often repetitious with Oracle-like statements that are not clear. Because the analysand is going through a transformation in his life, the new material and conscious attitude that is evolving will not make sense to the analysand during his active imagination process. It probably won't make sense when his therapist attempts to decode the dialogue. And it may take years until the analysand feels the truth of it. For example TCM says he is "awareness of the spirit" and leads me to the mystery of the basement. In other words my transformation depends on giving up my ego control and fear of my shadow and the spirits of the archetypal forces that comprise the totality of my Self.

There is enough powerful and symbolic truth in this active imagination piece to spawn an entire book, which in essence is this book. I chose *Frankenstein* as the springboard for the analytical concepts because it is more engaging literature than my dreams and active imaginations.

A significant metaphor in the dream is the eight steps. Carl Jung in his book, *Aion,* and Robert Moore in his series, *King, Warrior, Magician, Lover,* connect the number eight with the four sides of the male and female psyches that make up the eight-sided totality of the Self. I am called at mid-life to descend into the basement room (go into the unconscious) for eight steps to integrate shadow contents that include the masculine and feminine totality of my Self.

The TCM is an excellent character of shadow potential. Discovery of the TCM and dialogue with him parallel the journey taken by Victor Frankenstein with his monster. The TCM answers the question of what "split" he represents. "The power of the left behind" describes precisely the libidinous contents of the shadow. It is energy available for use as good or evil. The TCM says he could be my friend and complains that I have been "punishing" him and calling him a "demon" when he isn't.

One receives many instructions from parents. One is told, "Don't kick the dog" or "Don't pick your nose." Introjections from parents do not become shadow elements if one has no libido for the activity. But unlived potentials become encrypted into an unconscious being that waits for the opportunity to bring the potential into experience.

I assumed the TCM was evil and I was terrified of him. This is the ego's attitude toward its shadow. Victor Frankenstein has an identical reaction to his monster. The TCM is lonely and only minimally angry about being hidden away. The TCM tells me that his coat is a "mystery." Without his coat, he is "naked, a man." Nakedness is vulnerability. A two-year-old has no sense of a "flasher," but the implication is my two-year-old really wants to flash his shadow. A Freudian might misinterpret the image as repressed sexuality related to toilet training.

In the introduction one metaphor of *Re-Membering Frankenstein* is the repetitive nature of the monster's attempts to get our attention. The TCM remembers all, asks to be re-membered, and like Victor's monster, repeatedly attempted to engage my ego for years.

The basement room has lightness and darkness, i.e., good and evil energy. During active imagination I discovered a welcoming cadre of friends, personality fragments that were excluded from my persona.

Victor beams proudly as the monster rises from the workroom table. The moment of animation gratifies his scientific hubris. Victor's initial pleasure quickly degrades into horror. His first encounter ends, like my initial terror from the TCM, with Victor abandoning the monster.

Symbolic of Victor's neglected emotional and relationship needs, the monster has yellow skin and opens his "dull yellow eye." Yellow is the color of bile, a foreboding of the anger and destruction to come. His hair and lips are lustrous black, the hue of the shadow.

"I had worked hard for nearly two years, for the sole purpose of infusing life into an inanimate body. For this I had deprived myself of rest and health. I had desired it with an ardour that far exceeded moderation; but now that I had finished, the beauty of the dream vanished, and breathless horror and disgust filled my heart."

(Chap 5, par 3)

Victor's great scientific hubris creates a huge monster, i.e., the stronger the ego the more powerful the shadow becomes in balance. When we are boastful and reckless, others see our hubris immediately. Amazingly friends tolerate and forgive our pride despite their loathing of it. Victor's exuberance with his creation quickly turns to horror. This is equivalent to the time when a man realizes the effort he put into his persona and career has left him depleted and disgusted.

My personal realization occurred at age thirty-six sitting on my therapist's couch. While whimpering that all my education and planning had led me to misery and unhappiness, I came to grips with the fact that I had used my talents for greed and accumulation of wealth with insufficient caring for those around me.

Like Victor's laboratory monster that is pieces from multiple men, his inner monster has multiple sources. It contains the discarded parts of his feeling function. His father has rejected his natural inclination for the spiritual healing in alchemy. His individual freedom has been subjected to the culture of Geneva and his hand-me-down religion. Victor is expected to be a faithful Christian. His personal inner spirituality is not allowed. Sexual inclinations are prohibited by society and he is expected to remain chaste for Elizabeth. Duty to his parents has pushed Victor to become an agent of his family and culture. A powder keg of libido is now under the control of an inner monster.

The laboratory monster has no verbal language at creation; he cannot talk; he only groans. The TCM had no verbal communication being the shadow of a pre-verbal two-year-old. A feeling creature such as the Victor's monster communicates through image and action before he acquires language. The shadow's absence of language is partly the result of being established within the psyche at a pre-language stage, but primarily because it is an archaic psychic organ that evolved prior to formal language using primitive emotional pathways in the brain.

The Frankenstein images that are the foundations for this book occurred early in my psyche. At age nine I dreamt:

> *I am in the basement of my farmhouse and there is a non-functioning antiquated bar area in one corner. I look behind the counter and out walks Frankenstein.*

In my dream the creature is living behind the counter, that outer place where we service people, in my basement, my unconscious. And the monster is huge! I am four feet tall and my inner monster is already eight feet. I scream and run, grateful to escape by awakening back into the ego world.

As children we are all Victors who are too young and terrified to deal with our monsters. Hugeness is part of the shadow being. The Trench Coat Man was huge compared to my two-year-old. Fear of the monster's hugeness causes the ego to flee until the ego is large enough (mature and organized) to confront the monster. An effective confrontation with the monster is rare for a man younger than thirty-five.

An aspect of the shadow is that as it develops so does one's persona in proportion of opposite traits. I liken it to the image of Janus, the two-faced god, with one face looking forward and one backward. This gives the persona an inauthentic quality. We often recognize the persona/monster duplicity of others; and they easily see the phoniness of our persona. Our friends know what we are covering up. For example, my shadow is a reservoir for my aggression and violence; meanwhile, my outer persona appears sweet and innocent. My aggression comes through as sarcasm, and my friends know I'm no milk toast. Several television personas of evangelical ministers have had their shadows revealed as homosexuality drug abusers.

Persona contents that originate from family or cultural dictates are equally ingenuous. An insidious expectation of our patriarchal world order is to honor, obey, and exalt our fathers. Honoring one's personal father may take many forms. For example, the Ford family, like many ritual kingships, exerts an inexorable expectation that sons lead the family corporation. Prince Charles and his son, William, have no family-approved vocations other than the duties of the British royal family. Their souls are blocked; they are limited to the role of the archetypal king. Their personas do not hide the hardened sadness of their faces.

Parental expectations may match a child's Self's agenda. If so, it is heavenly. If Prince William's psyche desires to be king then he will likely have a reign of ease and experience fulfillment. However, if his Self has an agenda opposed to being king, his inner monster will act out, producing personal or societal calamity. Princess Diana's life exemplifies the agony of a Self denied. By most accounts, her soul was not comfortable with the role of princess.

Many men are born with rigid cultural and family instructions for a specified life course. A curse is to have no recourse from the pre-scripted life. Often this involves perpetuating a feud such as being an insurgent in the political struggles of the community. Northern Ireland, the Middle East, and most of Africa are places where millions of sons of political families act out the family curse by being a political warrior. The external demands upon these men create outer personas that are hideous monsters when viewed from the inner center of their Selfs. Hamlet is a fictional prince so cursed. Factories and office buildings house many men with long faces of flat affects whose souls have been abducted by outer forces.

Victor's first response to seeing the monster is to turn away and attempt to sleep. This is a regressive attempt to return to the state of denying the monster.

> **"Unable to endure the aspect of the being I had created, I rushed out of the room,...threw myself on my bed in my clothes...I slept."**
>
> **(Chap 5, par 3)**

Victor's denial fails; his unconscious persists by sending Victor wild and vivid dreams. Dreams are a forum for dialogue between the Self and the ego. In therapy, the dream content of the analysand is the most direct path toward wholeness of the Self because dream images derive from the Self and have minimal contamination from the therapist.

Victor dreams of a meeting with Elizabeth during which he kisses her:

> **"I embraced her; but as I imprinted the first kiss on her lips, they became livid with a hue of death, her features appeared to change, and I thought that I held the corpse of my dead mother in my arms; a shroud enveloped her form, and I saw the grave-worms crawling in the folds of the flannel."**
>
> **(Chap 5, par 3)**

The dream portends death to Elizabeth unless he can work the worms out of his situation. Victor's analyst would encourage his inner work, using this dream to help Victor discover that his attempts to bring his mother back to life were honest tries at reconnecting with his unconscious feeling function. The analyst would help Victor see that reconnection requires withdrawing maternal projections and integrating them into consciousness. Victor's dream says he has transferred his mother-complex function onto Elizabeth and warns that the process is turning Elizabeth into his mother and subsequently into a corpse. Although Victor agreed to marry Elizabeth at his mother's request, the dream suggests that kissing her (accepting her as his wife) is an act of holding onto his dead mother.

Victor's nightmares are just beginning. As he awakens from the dream the actual monster is at his bedside lifting up the bed curtain like an inquisitive toddler as if to say, "Good morning, Daddy." Victor screams in terror and runs out of the house. He cannot contain the monster image and regresses into flight!

Running may mean a physical escape or it may take the form of a quiet promise to never again commit monstrous deeds. When guilty, we all look for an exit. Running may mean suicidal thoughts. It may mean abandoning a marriage or job that reminds the man of his monster aspects. The logic has a component of face-saving blame: "They are making me into a monster, and I must change my job, spouse, or residence." Victor's logic is that the monster is the evil one, not he who created the monster. Victor abandons the creature, but his running from the house is a temporary escape. His monster problem cannot be solved without conscious input because the abandoned monster becomes autonomous and dangerous.

We need compassion for ourselves and for Victor. On the occasion when we do glimpse a monstrous commission, we naturally turn away. At nine or even twenty-nine I was unable to contain the horror of realizing how much potential monsterism resided within my psyche. I remember stealing a microphone from the junior high school in ninth grade. I was alone in study hall in the gymnasium. At that time in my life I was dabbling with music and I had joined a local rock-and-roll combo. I noticed a large microphone in the back corner of the stage. Before I could even reflect on the pros and cons of stealing, my inner thief seized me. In an almost out-of-body experience, I watched my hands snatch the device. To this day, my conscious serves up guilt over this incident.

My monster's impulsive capacity for perpetration was unsettling. One feels helpless knowing that a monstrous inner agency can seize the body and commit offenses, because he lacks the skill to constrain this force. I wanted to run away, to hide in shame. Like Victor, I naively hoped this event was aberrational and would not re-occur. Victor abandons the monster to spend the night out in the courtyard hoping his horrific creation will just disappear. He is like the boy who hides his disappointing report card from his parents. Victor is markedly distraught:

> **"I passed the night wretchedly.... Mingled with this horror, I felt the bitterness of disappointment; dreams that had been my food and pleasant rest for so long a space were now a hell to me; and the change was so rapid, the overthrow so complete!"**
>
> **(Chap 5, par 5)**

Welcome to the hell of midlife, Victor! Join us who have experienced the cruel irony that the energies poured into our successful careers have brought us emptiness and resentment. Attaining ego goals does not sustain the Self.

I reached the pinnacle of my career in my late thirties. I had overcome my impoverished childhood through focused studies in college and medical school. I had put aside pleasurable activities of sports, writing, card games, novel reading, and creative pursuits. I did not have time for extended friendships and relationships. Professionally I was at the height of my professional capabilities as department chairman; and my income was peaking. I had a new house and two lovely children. Delivery trucks were unloading material goods. The joy of a new speed boat lasted through two summers. I had achieved success, but was I happy?

I played some golf, but treated it as a competitive ordeal. When I played well I felt exalted; when I played poorly I was irritable and depressed. I did not sense my inner soul, shadow, or anima. I was feeling progressively dead to life.

I wasn't merely unhappy; my life had turned to hell! My marital relationship was an emotional toxic swamp. Despite the ease in which I could identify my spouse's faults, I was blind to my own. Yet I knew I was to blame for a good share of our joint misery. Sound familiar?

Life was purposeless. I wanted to stay married for my children's sake, but I couldn't imagine living with the monster that *my wife* had become. I was a typical unhappy man projecting my monster onto my spouse. The great hurdle of couples' therapy is to separate the genuine faults of one's spouse from the monster attributes one projects upon his/her spouse.

A man's monster projection may cause him to call his wife a witch. If an angry feminine witch resides inside of a man's psyche, it will appear to him in his woman partner. My personal anima/feminine feeling function was furious because I had neglected her (the anima is always a "her") desire to be deeply connected to friends and family. As a result my angry feminine saw my wife as angry. Meanwhile she was dealing with her inner masculine monster projected onto me. Marriage therapists observe this dyadic psychic combat daily.

The importance of transforming an angry inner feminine (anima) in a man cannot be overstated. Murder-suicides reported almost daily are the tragic end for hopeless men unable to transform the anger they project onto their spouses. Decoding dreams about murder victims is imperative for angry analysands. For example:

> There has been a murder of Nancy Sinatra in a wooded secluded area of upscale homes. The dreamer is part of a group of investigators. The dreamer suggests it might be related to her father's connections with the mafia. The dreamer discovers tracks in the snow that lead to a car. The killer is a skin-head fascist who has placed her head in the car. He pushes the dreamer alongside the head on the driver's seat and orders the dreamer to "tell them." ("them" refers to the police). The dreamer feels he is being set up to be blamed for the murder.

In this dream the dead female killed by a fascist represents his anima. That Nancy Sinatra's head is in the dreamer's car means she is still part of his psyche. The dreamer's ego fears being accused of a murder his ego denies committing, but he is actually responsible for a metaphor of murder, the suppression of his anima. The dreamer associated Nancy Sinatra with being a spoiled brat of entitlement, his devaluation of his anima. The dreamer was unaware that he similarly devalues his wife (Nancy is headless) and he has potential to harm her. The Mafia hit men who are connected with her father represent the pathology of the father-complex. The analyst should be prepared to receive a rebuttal or denial when he suggests this interpretation to the analysand. Also unlikely is that the analysand will associate his wife with the dream image of his anima.

Consider the following active imagination of the opposite problem. This man had a dream figure that looked like his wife but she tells him repeatedly that she is not his wife:

D: You are my wife, right? You look like her.
A: No, I am not your wife; I am Anna.
   (Anna may be a pun to sound like anima.)
D: Anna, if you are not my wife why did you leave me in the dream?
A: Because you are a fat pig asshole.
D: Is that the part you like?
   (The dreamer uses a sarcastic tone.)
A: Fuck you, you arrogant shithead. Make fun of me and I'll kill you, you cocksucker.
D: Why are you angry?
A: You talk to everyone else but me.
D: Ok, then talk.
A: You're too disgusting.
D: Wait a minute. I won't have you swearing and yelling at me if you won't talk. That's too much like my real wife.
A: Fuck you, fuck you, fuck you!
D: Ok, get it all out.
A: You treat me so badly, I want out of here.
D: Where?
A: Your body.
D: Is that possible?
A: Unfortunately no.
D: What bothers you the most?
A: Your blankness. How fucking detached and unfeeling you can be.
D: I'm sorry. You bring me tears.
A: Drown, you fucker.
D: I think that if you were gentler, maybe I'd talk to you more.
A: Fuck you.

D: When you say, "fuck you," I get mad at your blowing me off. Like you should have complete control. You are a tyrant.

A: Fuck you. I just want my fair share.

D: Of what?

A: Life!

D: Can you define that for me?

A: Aliveness, tingling excitement.

D: Dad gets in the way?

A: That old cocksucker, he should have killed you when he died. Only half the problem is dead.

D: Maybe you should talk with him also?

A: Fuck you, asshole. I wish I could kill the lot of you. But I suppose you could be right. I took so much shit from that fucker growing up and he's still living here. I wish I could kill the lot of you.

D: Is that why he died young?

A: Fuck him, I'm talking to you, you little pimp.

D: Like you're an angel, miss fuck everybody.

A: Fuck you, I'm tired. Goodbye.

Whew! That's one angry anima. The intensity of anima anger is commensurate with the degree to which the dreamer has repressed his feelings. She is willing to kill (suicide) this man and his father too, although the father is already dead. A helpful therapist will encourage the dreamer to continue engaging this anima figure; as she is listened to and respected, she will become more civil. She has been denigrated since the dreamer's childhood by his father-complex. Notice the dreamer's projection when he says he'd talk to her more if she were 'gentler;" he is insensitive to her. If the dreamer does not gain consciousness about his inner angry feminine, he will continue to project it upon his wife and do battle with her. This is the psychological setup for a murder-suicide of wife and husband; but he can avoid this tragedy by paying attention to his anima. Although the anima resembles his wife, she insists her name is different, specifically telling him that she is inside him and cannot leave.

I experienced anger from two inner sources: my anima and my monster. My ego-driven outer life and persona achieved success at the expense of inner life from which I had run away. Ironically it was the success itself that forced me to face my inner world. Reaching the top of the career mountain with goals accomplished meant that my ego-driven ambition had fizzled away. I found the mountain top to be an un-inhabitable ice-covered crest. Like Victor my inner monster was waiting there in the snow to confront me. Unaware that I needed to engage my inner monster, I waged emotional combat with my wife. Fighting the wrong demons causes many of life difficulties.

Fortunately the psyche has a remarkable capacity for renewal and healing. Opportunity for such renewal arrives for Victor. He is out wandering the next morning after abandoning his monster when who should arrive by "diligence," a public stagecoach, than his friend, Henry Clerval. This is fortuitous and hope-inspiring. Henry brings a different viewpoint, the inferior function's pleasure in the sensate joys of life.

Henry's appearance would be described by some as synchronicity, a meaningful coincidence in the outer world that corresponds with the inner landscape of the psyche. Some regard synchronicity as divine intervention. Regardless of the origin of synchronicity, when a meaningful metaphor crosses our path, the Self engages our attention so that we do take notice.

The name, Henry, connotes a ruler. Clerval is a combination of cler, meaning clear, and val, meaning valor or true. Henry carries the expressive power and desires of Victor's inner shadow figures. Henry is Victor's valet, a servant, who has come to Ingolstadt to nurse Victor back to psychological health. Metaphorically Henry represents the innate healing potential of balancing one's life. Henry leads Victor on long walks through nature. He reconnects Victor with pleasure of friendship and joy of nature. The unconscious is always attempting to find an outer community for our inner characters. As the psyche brings Henry's healing activities into service, the essential question becomes: Can Victor get in touch with his inner "Henry" in time to save his soul?

"Nothing could equal my delight on seeing Clerval; his presence brought back to my thoughts my father, Elizabeth, and all those scenes of home so dear to my

recollection...I felt suddenly, and for the first time during many months, calm and serene joy."

(Chap 5, par 9))

"Recollection" has several significant meanings. To re-collect can mean to collect again, thus connoting the potential for Victor to reassemble the disconnected components of his psyche. Recollection also implies meditation and calmness. One is said to relax and recollect himself. It sometimes refers to a recovery from illness. Victor feels instinctively that the presence of Henry has a healing effect on his soul.

Victor asks Henry how he came to the University. Henry states that he persevered in begging his father to allow him to study the calling of his heart: literature and arts. Henry's father acquiesced but held steadfast that:

"I have ten thousand florin a year without Greek, I eat heartily without Greek."

(Chap 5, par 9)

Henry is an important ingredient in Shelley's recipe of a healthy soul. Henry consciously names his desires and persists in fulfilling them without going crazy or acting out spontaneously. He is an example of escaping the grasp of the personal and the collective father-complexes.

The curse of living out one's father's life is the basis for many stories. In the movie, *Fingers*, a pianist son of a Mafioso boss is challenged to pursue the music of his soul's desire rather than his father's career as a gangster. Michael Corleone in the *Godfather* series loses his soul when he acquiesces to run his father's criminal empire. Hamlet must choose "to be or not be" true to his heart and marry Ophelia or to revenge his father's death. The simple wisdom of Joseph Campbell, mythologist, Jungian, and college professor, is to "follow your bliss!" Henry follows his bliss when he rejects his father's pressure to pursue the commercial importation business. In contrast to Henry, Victor is still engrossed in his study of science to please his father and Professor Krempe.

While Victor is elated by Henry's reviving presence, he is filled with trepidation that the monster might re-appear. When Victor searches the apartment and is fully convinced the monster has gone, he is giddy with relief and has a spontaneous outburst of joy.

> **"I jumped over the chairs, clapped my hands, and laughed aloud. Clerval...saw a wildness in my eyes for which he could not account; and my loud, unrestrained, heartless laughter, frightened and astonished him."**

> **(Chap 5, par 14)**

Henry comments that Victor is acting strangely and inquires why. We intuitively know that our best and closest friends can readily see our shadows. Victor immediately experiences guilt and becomes paranoid, suspecting that Henry knows about his monster creation. He lapses into a near psychotic breakdown of guilt:

> **"He can tell. 'Oh, save me! Save me!' I imagined that the monster seized me; I struggled furiously, and fell down in a fit."**

> **(Chap 5, par 16)**

Henry, unaware of Victor's activities, is understandably perplexed by Victor's shift from exuberance to despair. Victor, physically exhausted from his workaholic devotion to the monster creation, collapses. Exhaustion is an external manifestation of the enormous energy required to maintain an inflated ego. Henry begins nursing Victor back to health, and suggests Victor return home to visit Elizabeth and his father.

The un-expressed parts of the unconscious are continuously attempting to restore balance and joy, and are most likely to get the ego's attention when one is exhausted or defeated. Victor calls himself a miserable wretch, but Henry provides encouragement. The salutary influence of Henry leads to an upturn in Victor's health.

> **"I remember the first time I became capable of observing objects with any kind of pleasure, I perceived that the fallen leaves had disappeared, and that the young buds**

> **were shooting forth from the trees that shaded my window.**
> **It was a divine spring; and the season contributed greatly**
> **to my convalescence."**

(Chap 5, par 20)

Although Victor ascribes his improved health to pleasant spring weather, it is more accurate to say that he is able to enjoy the spring because of a healing respite from his studies. Jung, Johnson, and Edinger write that a person's joy enters through the inferior function. Victor's "divine spring" is his inner wellspring of joy bubbling up via his inferior function of sensation experienced through Henry.

Victor's delight in springtime is fleeting, as moments of ecstasy cannot be sustained. In the western mythic tale of the Holy Grail, moments of ecstatic joy are come-and-go experiences for Parsifal. He enters and loses the experience of the Grail Castle multiple times. The Grail Castle is a metaphoric place of spiritual bliss where one experiences moments of grace. No one can live continuously in bliss. Thrill seekers and new-age wanderers seek fruitlessly for unending bliss. The Grail Castle comes and goes because it is a place that can be permanently inhabited only by gods, not by humans. We increase our Grail Castle experiences as we increase contact with our inferior functions.

NOTES FOR CHAPTER 5

1. The monster or shadow is an organ of the psyche. It is born or created in images and feelings so early in life that it is often not verbal.

Question: What is your earliest desire that was denied to you and that you resent having to abandon?

Question: Can you remember what enraged you as a two-year-old?

2. Early encounters with one's monster incite horror and a desire to flee. The initial response to one's monster is to attribute evil to him.

106

Question: Can you recall a moment of horror when you discovered your capacity for destructive vengeance or other evil actions?

3. An obstacle for men in initiating therapy is altering their ego-controlled personas.

Question: Are you aware of persona attributes that consume an exhausting amount of your energy to maintain?

4. A man endangers his love relationship when he projects his anima/feminine feeling function on his female partner. Anger with women originates from an angry the inner feminine.

Question: What actions by your spouse/female/significant-other immediately get your goat and incite anger in you?

5. Active imagination is a valuable tool to dialogue with shadow figures while consciously awake. The process allows shadow monster expression of necessary libidinous contents.

Task: Conjure up an evil dream figure that has chased you or threatened you in some way. Engage in a conversation with this figure to discover why it wishes to interact with you.

6. An important shadow aspect is our inferior or least used function. It is the area of psychic functioning that we have the most difficulty accessing. It requires a conscientious effort to experience it. The inferior function is a conduit for the flow of our joy.

Question: What activities do you find joyous, but often avoid: such as social functions, creative activities, dancing, etc.?

7. The Self is vigilant in finding opportunities for renewal. An unconscious awareness within the Self will direct your attention to events, books, and persons who can best assist your transformation.

Question: What induced you to read this book?

CHAPTER 6

After three months of caregiving, Henry decides Victor is energetic enough to read his accumulated letters from home. Elizabeth writes that she is elated that Henry Clerval's magic is working. Victor's aging father requests Victor visit Geneva so he and Elizabeth might witness his improvement firsthand. Actually they are less worried about his health and more concerned that Victor's commitment to settle down and marry Elizabeth may be waning.

"Going home" is a metaphor for re-connecting with the unconscious. Going home in therapy implies sorting through family complexes. The letters are reminders that, although Victor is physically away from home, he has not escaped his father-complex, mother-complex, and anima. His father's request makes Victor antsy and irritable; and he retreats back to his science studies. Visiting his home re-activates family complexes. Many persons become anxious or irritable just contemplating going home, or having parents visit them. For others like Victor, home is imagined to be a pleasant nostalgic retreat, but they still avoid visiting and experiencing the falseness of their fantasy. What Victor needs is a compassionate but firm analyst to encourage him to strengthen his ego sufficiently to confront his father.

A side-story concerning Justine Moritz is presented in one of

Elizabeth's letters. Justine is a servant who came to work in the Frankenstein household after losing her father. Justine despised her natural mother and had a mutually loving relationship with Victor's mother. Justine's character, like Elizabeth, re-expresses Mary Shelley's fantasy of being rescued by an ideal stepmother. Elizabeth's description of Justine's love for Victor's mother reactivates Victor's mother-complex. He becomes maudlin, another example of how images or memories can instantly re-activate a dormant complex.

Elizabeth's letter next describes Victor's little brother, William.

> **"Sweet laughing blue eyes, dark eyelashes, and curling hair. When he smiles, two little dimples appear on each cheek, which are rosy with health..."**
>
> **(Chap 6, par 8)**

William is the divine child that everyone adores much like the spring flower, sweet william. The divine child image carries our innocence and innate desires free from judgment. Mary Shelley's father and son were both named William, her name of choice for an idealized lovable male.

I recall reconnecting with my divine child when I returned home after college graduation. Next door lived two schoolteachers and their precious little boy of five. That summer several times weekly I would walk with him into town for ice cream. He was so adorable I simply could not resist having him at my side. During my transition from college to medical school this synchronistic experience revitalized my inner child connection, at a time when intense career studies were making me stiff and serious. Victor re-experiences his inner child when reading about William.

Elizabeth's letter also contains a gossipy litany of maidens who have managed undeservedly to become engaged and are planning weddings. This is a not-so-subtle hint that Elizabeth is getting impatient about marriage. Recall that Mary Wollstonecraft at age seventeen ran off with Percy Shelley and became pregnant twice out of wedlock. Perhaps Elizabeth was expressing Mary Shelley's impatience to marry during the early months of writing *Frankenstein* while attending to her infant son, William. Surely the question of whether Percy, when he was no longer married, would wed Mary was in the minds of both as they lived together in Switzerland.

Marriage is a metaphor for the discovery, appreciation, and integration of the feminine aspects of a man. If Victor stays the course of Henry's directed recovery, he may achieve an outer and inner union of the masculine and feminine. The letter concludes with Elizabeth describing how writing has brought her peace and uplifted her spirits. Because Elizabeth is carrying Victor's feeling functions, she does feel better when she unburdens herself of feelings he should be experiencing.

Responding to Elizabeth, Victor recounts how Henry sensed Victor's discomfort with his science studies, correctly intuiting Victor's over-studying as the cause of his ill health. Henry removed the books and equipment from his room and laboratory, and marshaled Victor about Ingolstadt to experience the blossoms of spring.

Victor backslides from his healing course when he introduces Henry to the science professors at Ingolstadt. Although he has avoided visiting his father, Victor's reconnection with his science mentors re-activates his father-complex. Henry shuns the science Krempe advises in lieu of studying oriental languages and Buddhist mysticism. Victor in contrast is seduced by the praise of his professors and returns to his compulsive laboratory studies. For the addiction-prone, this is relapse. Victor is back to his laboratory the moment his professors encourage him.

Early autumn snowstorms make the mountains impassable, which is a new excuse for Victor to delay his returning home. An interesting historical side-story is that in 1817 intense volcanic activity in Indonesia caused the northern hemisphere to have no summer and heavy snowfall early in autumn. Scientific historians refer to this year as a micro-ice-age. Shelley weaves this actual weather event into her novel. Victor had plenty of opportunities to visit home from May until the actual snows began in September. Too often analysands use inconvenient events in the outer world to conveniently avoid their inner work.

Henry becomes engrossed in studying Arabic and Persian literature and enjoys his extended stay in Ingolstadt. Victor could travel alone to Geneva, but uses Henry as another excuse to avoid the home visit. The winter passes and Victor, despite his work compulsion, is doing well in the company of Henry, a noteworthy reminder that we tend to become complacent when we start to feel better during therapy and recovery. Therapy itself can sometimes side-track us. Some patients become enamored with their therapy or their support groups and their progress plateaus. Analysands stuck in twelve-step programs are one example. Crusaders against domestic violence or child abuse can be similarly stuck. I've seen men so attached to drumming in men's groups that their personal and professional lives disintegrate.

Victor is at such a plateau. A taste of sensate pleasure has left him unwilling to confront his father's disapproval. But sensate pleasures are short-lived if not the result of conscious growth. A man may find a new hobby or a new career. He may run off with a younger woman. He may take up guitar and form a blues band. He may join a men's group and drum naked in the woods. In the seventies it was commonplace for businessmen to don Nehru jackets and wear gold medallions about their necks. Harley Davidson sells most of its new motorcycles to forty-something men who have "rediscovered" their inner adventurer. Whatever the newfound expression of inner sensate ecstasy, if an inferior function is not integrated consciously, it is doomed to be short-lived. Victor, having fused his sensation experience with the life of Henry Clerval, remains disconnected from the other dynamic "members" of his psychic committee; thus, he is setup for relapse into his compulsion.

NOTES FOR CHAPTER 6

1. Life balance is an important part of psychological health. For Victor it means freeing himself from his work addiction and experiencing his sensate function.

Question: What do you enjoy but cannot find time to do?

2. Joy comes to a man through his least accessible areas, his inferior functions. Take responsibility for your own joy. Beware of allowing

others to carry your inferior functions. For a man like Victor with a primary thinking function, joy is found in the sensate pleasures of nature, love, friendship, colors, scent, and sounds.

Question: What is your inferior function; and how is it expressed and repressed in you?

3. The healing nature of experiencing one's inferior function is short-lived until one consciously understands the need. Beware that we are prone to quick-fixes.

Question: What are your activities that bring short-lived joy?

4. Relapse is an expected part of the growth process.

A. Any simple image or event can trigger a complex.

B. Disasters and bad luck occur, but one must be diligent or he will invite his misfortunes.

Question: Can you name a pattern of events that disrupts the balance in your life? Family issues? Work demands? Losing a job?

5. We often develop compulsions or addictions to avoid inner reflection.

Question: In what activity do you compulsively engage to discharge libido?

CHAPTER 7

The spring thaw was complete a month ago and daffodils are blooming, but Victor continues to put off his home visit. His current excuse is that Henry loves to wander about the mountains enjoying the spring flowers. Besides avoiding his father, Victor is dawdling because he cannot face Elizabeth with a conviction to marry her. The movie, *Arthur,* is a comical version of the same dilemma. Arthur, played by Dudley Moore, drinks compulsively to avoid his family and the fiancé they arranged for him.

A therapeutic maxim warns that putting off inner work invites greater pain. Victor's procrastination brings disaster. Victor receives news from his father that his youngest brother, William, has been murdered! Mary Shelley wrote this at the time her son, William, was a toddler at her feet, probable evidence she feared he might die like her first premature baby.

William was found strangled. Elizabeth is aggrieved and blames herself for the demise of her brother. She had given William her necklace with a locket containing a picture of his deceased mother to wear. The locket is missing and theft is presumed to be the murderer's motive.

Death of the divine child is a significant loss for men. We recognize this dead function in adult men who angrily disdain frail boys. They value competitive sports, business, politics, and especially war. Life becomes a hyper-vigilant serious job. They have trouble relaxing in the moment. If they engage in sports, betting and winning are all important. It is not joyous play. They hate the "chick-flick" movies of emotional attachments. They fail to sense the awe of nature. They prefer drilling oil wells on beaches to sunbathing. They live by the credo, "Life sucks and then you die."

Fathers accelerate the death of the innocent child when they push sons to grow up and take on adult responsibility prematurely, or become warriors who "fight back" at the slightest provocation. In contrast the Puer aeternus, or Peter Pan flyboy, is a young man who refuses to adapt to the adult father world. Peter Pan wishes to remain a boy at perpetual play in Never-(an adult)-Land. The humorless workaholic is the polar opposite; he cannot sustain the freshness and joy of childhood. A conscious and mature ego will strike a balance between work world and play. With a balanced psyche a man can fulfill adult responsibilities while retaining contact with his joy-filled child.

Men who are experiencing a pathologic distance from their inner child will present in therapy with dreams of lost or dead children or young boys trapped in wells or mines underground.

> *The dreamer is a boy in his bedroom at his parent's house. He sees a lost boy out in the back yard. He is afraid the boy will see the dreamer's body, so the dreamer pulls the covers over himself except for his face.*

The boy in the back yard represents the dreamer's inner child. The lost child wants the dream ego to let him into his house (his life). The dream occurs in his parent's house, i.e., the dreamer is under control of his parental-complexes. He is trying not to let the backyard boy see him, i.e., his ego is excluding his inner child. The dreamer feels shame of exposing his body to the boy, i.e., the lost embodiment of the child's feelings. Keeping his face in view is "saving face," i.e. preserving the ego's persona.

Here is another dream of the inner child seeking expression in the dreamer's consciousness.

The dreamer is babysitting a small infant about ten months old. He is well behaved and playing quietly in his high chair. Suddenly he announces,"I'm hungry. I've been up since 9:30." The dreamer tries to give him some cornflakes but cannot get the package open.

This dream is humorous in that the well-behaved boy is ten months old but can talk. He is getting impatient and needs nourishment. We sense that this toddler will become a little monster if further ignored. The dreamer cannot get the cornflakes open. He needs assistance in nurturing his inner child.

Dreams of small children in various predicaments are a clue that the analysand requires re-acquaintance with the libido of his inner child. The following dream is from a man with a traditional religious connection.

The dreamer is babysitting a four-year-old boy who he thinks is a nephew although the dreamer has none in actual life. Satan enters the room and the dreamer feels fear that Satan has come to steal the child. He draws a cross on Satan's back and pushes him out the door while saying the Lord's Prayer.

The Self is attempting to draw the attention to the inner child. Sin, as represented by Satan, pertains to losing the child. Associated with Satan, the dreamer confesses that he has viewed many aspects of childhood such as playfulness and natural bodily pleasures, including sexuality, as sinful. The dreamer/babysitter is responsible for the child. The child is "family" at the psychic level. The analysand at the time was re-configuring his spiritual thoughts to granting a personal divinity to the Self. The dream encourages the dreamer to compare the evil projection upon Satan to the ego's neglect of the divine child.

Divine child dreams summon the analysand to focus on the libido of the inner child with awe for life and knowledge. It is a source of kindness and respect for others, particularly the weak. The child carries a man's ability to play and share the simple joys of life with others. Therapists should anticipate resistance convincing the analysands of the value of saving the divine child. Resurrection is an arduous task. Victor needs time on the couch with his eyes closed to resurrect into consciousness his nature as a five-year-old boy.

I brought the following dream to my analyst:

> *I am a small boy living inside a large but normal human head. The front of the head opens like a garage door. I peer out from the head into a dark area. It seems as if I am looking out from the inside of a semi-trailer. I realize I am a five-year-old boy who is hesitant to walk out. As I peer out down the trailer cavity there is an intense god-like bright light at the end.*

We often dream about blocked areas in our lives. A clue to blocked topics is that a dream makes no sense. Hence, when I was bewildered with the dream, I didn't wait for my therapist to suggest that I engage this little child to decipher this dream.

I launched into an active imagination and brought this work to our next session. I understood nearly nothing of the content at the time, but I trusted that my analyst would help decode the information. I did this work in 1993 and years later I am humbled and awed at the wisdom and value of the exercise. My actual conversation is in italics; current comments are written in regular text.

Greg: Tell me about yourself, little five-year-old.

Greg has the correct attitude: inviting and respectful.

Boy: You can call me Tim. I am alive with the wonder of the world.

My analyst, Dr. Robert Moore, observed that the characters in dreams and active imagination are so much more direct and confrontational than any therapist would dare to attempt.

Greg: Are you afraid?

Tim: No, but naively vulnerable. Remember watching the sunrise from the couch as a grade-schooler? Recall the radiant warmth, the cold glass, and the snow that glittered on the fields across the street? You used to sit there in awe.

From ages 9-12 I had the habit of awakening about 4 AM and reading in the living room until dawn, then marveling at the sunrise. Note that Tim carries the sensate function in his descriptions. As a strong intuitive I have immense difficulty experiencing the sensate that is clearly my inferior function.

Greg: Yes, I knew there was another life out there that I couldn't quite reach. How are you stuck in my head?

When an analysand dreams of another outside himself (an alien, unfamiliar being, or god out there), it references a cut-off part of the Self.

Tim: I just sit here marveling at the world. Really I'm happy and content.

When attempting to loosen up a despondent analysand, it is sometimes helpful to encourage him to remember a time in his childhood when he was peaceful and content.

Greg: What became of you as I grew up?
Tim: The most painful time was early teens. You became misled by (name of a recalcitrant friend) and lost your artistic connection in drama class. Between him and your dad's disdain for the theater, you really lost an opportunity for connecting with your creative self.

The innocent child in us is vulnerable to family and peer pressures. Delinquency in adolescence is often an over-reactive attempt to suppress the inner child as a boy transitions to adulthood. This certainly was my story.

Greg: Yes, I was trying to be cool and get into sex. Do you know why I was so attracted to ….(list of four women's names)….who were so averse to sex?
Tim: You'll need to talk to the anima about that. She's the one working on that inner agenda.

Active imagination characters are real, honest, and remain in character. Notice that Tim has no sexual issues. He does not speak for other members of my inner the family and directs me to the anima.

Greg: Can you remind me of times when you asserted yourself?
Tim: I'm not really assertive.

Here again, Tim knows exactly who he is and who else resides in the unconscious, such as the trickster that he mentions in the next sentence.

Greg: *Any shadow things I should know about?*

Tim: *Sometimes I work with the trickster to do dangerous experiments, often with people. Even the pushing you do to your wife.*

Greg: *Do you see yourself as permanent or someone I need to change?*

Tim: *Oh, I need to grow up. My only protection so far has been inside this skull. I am amazed by the through-the-eyes garage door you've given me to escape.*

Tim resides in semi-trailer which is a transport or carrier of important goods. It travels until it is delivered into use, stored in the trailer of my head.

Greg: *Are you coming out?*

Tim: *I don't know. It's safe in here.*

Greg: *How about organizing the trash and artifacts about you?*

Tim: *That's not my job.*

Greg: *Maybe it would help you grow up.*

Tim: *I'd rather play.*

Greg: *Grownups can play, too. Tell me, do you feel abused or hurt in any way?*

Tim: *Yes, I am sad about the loss of playmates. I am really mad at my parents. Dad shamed me out of friends and wouldn't do what was necessary to allow me to play over at Joey or Robin's house. I so much loved to play with them. I wouldn't have become such a compulsive baseball fantasy loner if I could have played with them. I grew up without friends. Go ahead and cry/grieve. Mom didn't help much either. Remember the 5th grade party at Becky's house? How much fun we had? How much you loved the boys and girls? How you felt part of the group, not once striving to be one-up?*

Greg: *And I remember the ridicule I got when Mark sent me that "love letter" as dad and my brothers referred to it. Seems that whenever I had a friendship, I didn't have the resources to let it flourish. Do you remember the baseball game in fourth grade?*

Tim: "Hanging out" too long with inappropriate people was not in your best interests. (list of four names)

Tim is clear about being a child and valuing play. Further Tim harbors lingering pain over not enough play and playmates as a child. Tim identifies my loner fantasy baseball compulsion as an outlet for his libido. He chastises me for choosing inappropriate friends later in adolescence that signaled a rejection of his honest naiveté.

Greg: Most of my friends have good hearts, but also some evil near the surface. Is that because you, the five-year-old, don't recognize my evil?
Tim: It's a vicarious way of expressing your shadow. You experience your evil in others and forgive and love them.

Bingo, Tim lays it out clearly! Men use friendships for their vicarious needs. Victor uses his friendship with Henry to unconsciously siphon libido back from him. I was more likely to find mischievous friends to express my shadow. Tim reveals my lingering pain of too few friendships in our childhood that makes current intimacy more difficult.

Next I try to help Tim mature into an adult, but Tim is an archetype that does not change its essential nature.

Greg: Can you visualize yourself growing up or getting over not having boyhood friendships?
Tim: It's tough. If true friendships weren't blessed and supported and you hung out with borderline miscreants who eventually let you down, there isn't a good program for believing in people. Your parents and friends weren't helpful or supportive. You feel that letting yourself get too vulnerable will be disastrous.
Greg: Speaking of unhealthy relationships, I don't really get why I'm attracted to women who are so asexual.
Tim: Guaranteed safety! If you haven't had a sustained series of good friendships, you will be fearful, especially of involvement with women.
Greg: Is there some mother fantasy at work here?
Tim: The look on their faces! The affect on their faces says I'm hurt; help me. Like mom, get it? Remember that one morning when

mom was crying after fighting with dad? You were maybe six.
How painful that was to you.

At this I experienced an "ah hah" revelation that I have mother-complex and healer issues that affect my choices about women.

Greg: *So are you suggesting that my mother-complex and that*
becoming a physician are related?

Tim: *All healers have a wish to alleviate pain in others. That's noble*
as long as it is compassion-based and not a need to hide or deny
your own pain.

Greg: *Is there anything that you are hiding? Are there any really painful*
episodes of significance?

Tim: *The leg burn at age seven is probably the worst. I feared dying,*
being left alone to die, that nobody cared. The dream I had of
being left out on the roof to die alone. The experience of losing
one room-mate after another, as they were rapidly discharged,
was discouraging. I thought I'd never go home. Plus I never saw
any of those children again.

At age seven while making cat-tail torches dipped in gasoline,
I managed to inflict severe third degree burns on my left leg. I was
hospitalized for three months as the burns requiring skin-grafting. I
had severe infections and nearly died at one point. I suffered not only
physical but emotionally pain because the adults never explained what
was going on. Whenever I asked about being discharged, the staff
would answer with the lie, "Soon." I became hopeless and depressed.
One night I dreamt that my hospital bed had been wheeled out onto
the roof and I was abandoned to die.

Greg: *How do we do heal that? And don't say grieve! I can't just flip a*
grief switch.

Tim: *It is deeply embedded in the muscles. Take my hand, I'm ready*
to walk out now.

Greg: *Where?*

Tim: *Everywhere! I'll sit in the light right next to your heart. You will*
protect me, but I can guide your heart with the awe, wonder,
and honesty of a five-year-old---that's how we can have intimate
friends.

Greg: I wish I could weep out the heavy muscle pain. Do you think I can?

Holistic healers are better tuned-in to the bodily aspects of psychic pain than allopathic physicians. Ulcers, spastic colons, temporal-mandibular jaw pain from bruxism, migraines, back pains, etc. are often reservoirs for psychic pain. Awareness of pain locations associated with specific psycho-social origins is an important step in the relief of many somatic symptoms.

Tim: Have compassion for Mom and Dad, but don't let them off the hook. It's work worth doing. Sure, you can do it. This is insidious stuff, no dramatic abuse here, just a lost child.

Greg: God, the pain feels so close to the surface, but when I try to release it dives deep and far away.

Tim: Take a moment to reflect on the journey so far. The first phase was unleashing the massive heat of pain and resentment from the family. The next big plateau was giving yourself permission and power and assurance to continue facing other pains. Now we are into loosening up the deeper stuff, the tar over the natural Self. Think about your body. You now have the wings of the black pterodactyl warrior, the lion skin of the king, and the heart of the five-year-old.

This paragraph contains many personal images and events of my therapeutic process. The heat release refers to dreams I experienced early in therapy. In my first heart-pounding dream I opened the door of a blast furnace and released pent-up anger. Later I had multiple dreams of my childhood homes being burned by fires smoldering in the basement. Unconsciously I released anger and libido as therapy uncovered childhood pain. The pterodactyl was an image of my primitive libido and creativity. The lion skin I donned in a dream as I recaptured a sense of inner kingship. In this active imagination Tim has summarized my progress and encourages me to continue. I love that Tim ends the imagination just as a five-year-old child would do: he says he's tired and quits.

Greg: So don't we need to mature that image?

Tim: Let's start from there and see what happens. Enough! I'm worn out, Goodbye!

There is an abundance of wisdom in this process of active imagination. Dr. Moore advised that I talk again to this Tim character saying, "He is extremely wise and straightforward and much cheaper than coming to me!"

Losing one's innocent child is a tragic loss. Men who are tough, grumpy, or cold as ice have suffered this loss. Many shouting radio and TV pundits have lost contact with their inner child. Victor's neglect of his inner child during compulsive work is imaged in William's death; Victor can regain his passion for life if he can reconnect with the boy who is lost in his unconscious.

En-route to William's funeral in Geneva, Victor expresses grief and despair. The Alps now appear black to him and the lakes, a deep fathomless blue. He grieves that his absence from home for six years meant he only knew William through letters. He also grieves his neglect of Elizabeth. The memories of his own boyhood are a distant fog, as dead to his consciousness as William. On the outskirts of Geneva a storm breaks out over the mountains. Victor cries,

"William, dear angel! This is thy funeral, this is thy dirge!"

(Chap 7, par 25)

A lightning flash illuminates the presence of his created monster. Victor recognizes him by size and shape, but the monster scurries out of sight up the mountain trails. The monster appearing during Victor's grief is a hopeful sign. But Victor's ego is too small and immature to confront the monster; instead of greeting the monster, Victor runs away and shivers in terror.

Victor correctly deduces that the monster murdered his brother. The mother figure in the locket picture links his mother-complex via the monster to William's death. Victor's procrastination and detachment from his monster has provoked his monster to commit murder. His immediate incapacitating concern is how to avoid blame for creating this murderer. This is "face-saving," the act of preserving the ego-invested persona, like the dreamer who pulled the covers over his body. Victor tries unsuccessfully to console himself. He cannot get the image of the monster out of his mind. Victor laments his creation.

> **"I considered the being whom I had cast among mankind, and endowed with the will and power to effect purposes of horror, such as the deed which he had now done, nearly in the light of my own vampire, my own spirit let loose from the grave, and forced to destroy all that was dear to me."**
>
> **(Chap 7, par 27)**

Victor has reached the devastating moment in a man's life when he realizes that he harbors a hideous, unimaginably ugly, and death-producing monster. A monster lives within him, it is not going away, and he cannot run away from it. Shelley implicates a vampiric nature to Victor's monster. Typical dream images of the inner monster are vampires, aliens, Nazis, or violent criminals.

> *The dreamer is in an old house with several other men who he realizes are vampires that intend to bite him into an eternity of vampirism. They begin to bite the dreamer when the dreamer observes a young androgynous boy who refuses to be bitten. The vampires grouse and hiss but leave the boy alone.*

Here the dreamer's divine child contains his resistance to succumbing to the vampiric nature of the shadow. The vampire represents the part of him that sucks the libido out of the balancing aspects of his personality, specifically for this man, his inner child aspects.

> *The dreamer is at the Canadian border with an unknown man and woman. He has U.S. citizenship but the unknown couple is Canadian. They tell the dreamer to get into the boat and they will all cross the St. Lawrence River and sneak into the States. The dreamer knows they are lawbreakers but feels helpless as they drive the boat toward the border.*

This man's shadow is a composite of male and female aliens. They are coming into consciousness (in a boat on water) despite his terror and resistance. Terror is a clue of a shadow element the ego fears.

> The dreamer, while in the mountains, is approached by a scary group of space aliens. He begins a conversation with one seemingly nice man only to find out his agenda is to take over the entire group. The dreamer tries to stab the man but discovers he is invincible.

This dream educated the analysand about the immortal archetypal nature of the monster. It cannot be killed but must be transformed through consciousness.

> A dreamer is at a lakeside resort in an old guest house. There are ham, steaks, and other meats in the freezer which don't look right and are discolored. The dreamer looks closely and concludes the meat is poisoned. A raccoon eats a piece of meat and dies. Dogs steal some meat and they die also. An evil looking Aryan youth appears and is snickering. When confronted he neither admits nor denies tainting the meat. The Aryan youth chases the man into the lake. The dreamer in terror tries to swim away from the youth, but this creates additional fears of being eaten by giant fish in the lake.

The dreamer's shadow includes a saboteur who serves toxic meat. The dreamer is terrified at confronting the youth, i.e., his shadow. Being eaten by the big fish as in Pinocchio or the Jonah-whale stories is the fear of feeling inadequate to confront the unconscious. Confronting one's shadow is overwhelming and terrifying. This analysand needs help organizing enough ego strength to confront his unconscious. The Aryan youth chases the dreamer but the dreamer is unsure if he will poison him. In *Frankenstein* the monster is ambivalent whether to kill Victor but relentlessly pursues him.

The analysand in this dream was encouraged to dialogue with the Aryan youth saboteur in active imagination.

Dreamer: Can we talk about what you are doing in my life?
Saboteur: I am ventilating.

D: *Bringing air or airing anger?*

S: *Cutting the wimp out of you and your friends.*

(The Saboteur is pointing out the lack of libido in the dreamer's nice-boy persona. This man's shadow carries his aggression. Notice how he tried to swim away to avoid confrontation with the saboteur.)

D: *Perhaps you underestimate my resolve not to let you ruin my lives.*

S: *We'll see about that.*

D: *What troubles you the most?*

S: *Your cowardice.*

D: *Such as?*

S: *You don't stand up to anyone, particularly your wife.*

D: *Go on.*

S: *The poison meat is for you, your wake up call. Die or get it together.*

D: *I think you're the reason I eat too much.*

S: *Not me, that's the feminine food lady. All I want to do is choke you.*

The saboteur knows who he is: the masculine archetype of aggression, and not the archetypal character of addiction, the dreamer's "food lady."

D: *Another ventilation reference?*

S: *Don't get cute with me. I could be a useful friend.*

D: *For what?*

S: *Not being walked over at one of your good-little-boy parties.*

D: *How can I trust you have my best interests at heart?*

S: *You don't have a choice. Maybe I will save your life.*

D: *If so, why were you chasing me into the water?*

S: *I don't care if you die but I'm not going to.*

D: *I can't let you ruin my body.*

S: *That's your problem.*

D: *What can I do to make you a useful friend?*

S: *Open your heart and let me ride with you in the open. The point is that I can kill you, but if you keep me in the open and use me, then I can't sabotage you or others.*

This active imagination lays out the essence of this man's monster work. His monster has important libido: the capacity to kill, enact vengeance, or use aggression for appropriate protection. If a man can do active imagination with his monster, it will generally tell the man exactly what he must do. For the above man, he must use his aggression openly and appropriately without feeling guilty. The consequence of failure is that his monster will sabotage his joy.

Victor is about to get similar advice from his monster. The discovery of the monster's power and invincibility terrifies Victor. A therapist friend of mine recounted the moment he discovered his monster and its evil nature. On an airplane from Los Angeles to Chicago, he was overcome by the sinister deeds of his life and cried for the duration of the flight.

At age forty I had such a moment when I dropped in despair onto the floor of my bedroom closet. I wept in remorse for transgressions, rudeness, and other moral lapses. I was flooded with a litany of character flaws that made me feel unworthy to be alive. I wasn't suicidal but felt I was a wretch who deserved death. Victor can no longer deny the evil of his monster now that William is dead.

Accepting the vileness of your monster comes with the double whammy of simultaneously seeing the phoniness of your persona. A man's stomach will clench as he realizes that his persona is fake theatrical make-up. This may be the moment when a man admits to himself that he has chosen a profession or operated a business purely for profit and without soul. His lack of compassion haunts him in the faces of those he has cheated or exploited. He feels guilty for deeds for which there is no atonement. He becomes disoriented because the persona in the mirror is now intolerable.

Discovering the shadow and deconstructing the persona is often accompanied by dreams of shedding layers of clothes like peeling onion rings. Other images include being covered with excrement, engulfed in volcanic lava, drowning in a mudslide, or being dumped into a pool of some disgusting or toxic substance. It is a dangerous time when suicidal ideation is common. Men need assistance in containing this confrontation.

The revelation of the shadow is so unpleasant that the ego and persona increase their effort to distance themselves from the shadow.

Victor has the dilemma of exposing the monster or protecting his reputation. Although he knows that the monster murdered his brother, Victor capitulates to his fears that the townspeople might disbelieve the truth and think him insane for claiming to have created the monster.

Modern society lacks a collective container to assist a man with his shadow work. A man in midlife frequently feels he is going insane, and outwardly he may appear crazy. Hopefully his intra-psychic transformation will be a productive crazy period with no irreparable violence committed. Specifically a man needs the following resources. He needs the permission and blessing of the culture and his family to undertake his heroic midlife transition. He needs the time and the financial resources for therapy. Third, he needs tolerance for his apparent outward craziness until he establishes a new balance of his psyche.

NOTES FOR CHAPTER 7, Part I, Death of the Inner Child:

1. We have an archetypal inner child that carries a zest for being alive, a naïve quality of awe of the world, and a trusting appreciation. Our friends and family cherish our inner child.

Question: To what extent have you lost your zest for life, nature, sunsets, new friends, and the gentleness pace experiencing the present?

2. Loss of contact with one's inner child is often associated with excessive seriousness, combativeness, and disdain for children and the weak.

Question: What do you think about too seriously? Death? Money? Politics? Social decay?

3. The lost child is a shadow character related to the anima and the mother complex. It holds a great volume of feeling content.

Question: Can you take an adult situation and imagine experiencing it as a five-year-old?

4. Dreams of dead or endangered young boys are a sign of the lost inner child that is attempting to contact us.

Question: Can you recall a dream of an injured or imperiled boy?

5. Active imagination is a tool to uncover the agenda of the Self. It is useful to elicit what a dream character represents, identify issues to address, and locate where unconscious libido is currently residing, such as being carried by a friend.

Task: Close your eyes, image a boy dream character, and then dialogue with him. Ask his name, fears, hopes, and how he is part of you.

6. Psychic suffering may be localized in the body, a possibility when there is a chronic pain that cannot be medically explained.

Question: Do you have illnesses that are stress related?

7. The goal of inner child work is to re-connect with one's intrinsic personality that was present since birth and to allow the flow of joy, wonder, and connection with others.

Question: What joyous activities from childhood do you no longer pursue in your life?

8. Men are horrified when they discover their immutable shadows. These discoveries are associated with personal and social danger.

Questions: In confronting you inner monster, what experience do you identify as most horrific?

What fictional monster characterizes your personal monster?

Victor enters his home in Geneva before dawn while his family is asleep. Sleeping is a metaphor for his family's lack of awareness that Victor and his monster are responsible for William's death. Dawn occurs just prior to light (a metaphor for enlightenment).

Stopping in a hallway Victor sees a painting of his dead mother kneeling over her father's coffin, a powerful depiction of entrenched parental-complexes that linger even after the parents die. For Victor's family it showcases his mother's devotion to patriarchal values.

Multi-generational dreams imply active multi-generational parental-complexes.

> I am in my grandfather's garage. Parked there is my '58 Buick (a hand-me-down car from my father) but in the dream it belongs to my deceased dad. I see a dagger stuck in the right rear door. I ask my grandfather about the dagger and my father's health at the time of his death. There is an immediate whirling and deep spinning like an internal tornado into my body.

My analyst interpreted the dream as a trans-generational descent of the father-complex. The car was owned by my father and passed down to me. The family legacy is the dagger that is internalized in me indicated by the deep whirling when I ask about it. My father committed suicide in a garage inside another Buick he owned. The psychic injury represented by the dagger is insidious, in the right rear door.

I came from a line of unfeeling and harsh men. My father's rigid attitude contributed to his suicide at age forty-six; he refused to grant himself the permission necessary for mid-life transformation. Much of his pain was attributable to his sadistic father. I experienced my grandfather's sadism first hand. Once I was watching a baseball game at his house. My grandfather repeatedly switched the set off-and-on from a remote control to tease and frustrate me. I was unaware of the remote and expressed dismay and confusion. He laughed and said the TV just did that. Another time I accompanied him to a grocery where he worked part time. He ordered me to stand in a spot near a vicious barking dog. He enjoyed my terror. To this day I get an uncomfortable feeling just entering my childhood city, especially driving down the street where my grandfather lived.

Confronting the hall painting of his grieving mother activates Victor's parental-complexes. His mother lies dead six years, but her effect upon Victor is immediate. Although Victor has moved away, he has never done the inner work to protect him from the spell of his parental-complexes. Overcoming the curse of family pathology that passes through the generations is a true miracle of personal development.

Negative reaction to a complex often manifests by being overtaken with a bad mood. A seemingly innocuous statement can change one's affect from pleasant to sullen. Our wives and friends have witnessed this transformation in us. Maturity requires gaining awareness of the triggers. We will still reflexively snarl at the emotional content of a trigger, but with consciousness we can apologize and return to the present quickly enough to avoid a vitriolic escalation.

A typical boy feels his father to be the wisest, strongest, and most impenetrable force in his life. From the deep levels of our formative psyches we strive to emulate our fathers. The father-complex is displayed in imitation and idealization but from a child's viewpoint. As Victor contemplates the picture he thinks of his own father and emotionally regresses from super-scientist to subservient child. Many men blindly follow their fathers into medicine, law, politics, or the family business. "I never really considered another profession," they will often admit. Men are unaware that they are programmed to believe that being a real man requires imitating one's father. Taking on a father's profession honors the father and may be intrinsically rewarding and fulfilling for the son. However, millions of men suffer a life-long depression because their souls desire a profession different from their father.

An equaling distressing variant is a son entering the profession his father wanted but did not obtain. The son's psyche has a program that says: dad is a good man; dad wanted to be a lawyer; I should honor my father by becoming a lawyer, thus pleasing my father. Many professional athletes unconsciously are living out their father's unsuccessful athletic ambitions. Often their inner monsters revolt through drugs, gambling, or sexual promiscuity because their athletic vocations do not fulfill their intrinsic needs. I think Tiger Woods truly desires to be the best golfer ever and this was encouraged by his father, but a part of his repressed psyche, likely relationship suppression, has erupted in sexual promiscuity.

A physician in our medical community was a born storyteller, but he came from a family where the capable men were expected to become physicians. He was a poor physician because he was disinterested in medicine. His patients were poorly served. The physician was bored and longed to write books. He died from a heart attack at an early age, having lived too short a life under a family curse that directed him into medicine instead of following the calling of his soul.

QC, a man of fifty, is a lawyer who hates the practice of law. He thrived financially during the stock market explosion of the 1990's which allowed him to stop practicing law and work with investments. After the dot.com bubble burst he lost his new fortune and was forced to resume practicing law. He now battles suicidal thoughts. Saddest of all, his twenty-two-year-old son, a delightful young man who loves working with his hands, is applying to law school, thus carrying on their multi-generational father-complex-curse.

Anti-social behaviors are often passed to sons through multi-generational father-complexes. Common are legacies of violence, drunkenness, and criminal acts. The prisons house many young men who travelled the paths blazed by their fathers. This is more than simply following a bad example. These sons love their fathers. Emulating their fathers' criminal professions is an act of honoring their fathers. Such a son is praised either by his actual father or from an internal feeling of success via his father-complex. Going straight requires overcoming the guilt of being disloyal to their fathers.

"Real man" introjects begin in infancy. The son emulates his father to satisfy the universal need to feel masculine. A son also internalizes a critical judge of whether he is living up to his masculine ideal. If his internal masculine critic judges himself inadequate, depression may ensue. No amount of praise from his father or from other men alleviates the son's depression because the judge who matters most lies within his psyche. But the real father, who modulates the son's father-complex, can evoke the harsh internal judge by actual or perceived criticism of the son. Movies and books abound with the theme of the son who cannot get his father's blessing. The true cause of the son's misery is not that he cannot please his father, but that he cannot please his internal masculine judge.

Other ways a son may emulate his father are through social, political, and religious opinions and practices. Why do the Hatfields and McCoys perpetuate their feuds? Their repetitious acts honor the struggles of their fathers, driven by the common jingoistic shibboleth, "Lest our fathers died in vain, we must continue to fight their wars." In continuing the feuds, wars, and genocides, men are in effect praying at the altar of the god-image of the fathers.

The father-complex includes conscription to the cultural religion. The majority of active religions are patriarchal with god-images carried in the masculine side of the psyche for both men and women. The psyche of the son projects its inner god-image (the Self) onto the collective god-image. Killing in the name of Jesus, Allah, Jehovah, or Brahma is an expression of love and devotion to the male ancestry (collective father-complex). Its deep entrenchment makes peace impossible. The perpetual violence of warring societies cannot be stopped until sons allow themselves the possibility of not perpetuating their father's wars. The persistence of cultural wars for thousands of years attests to the power that multi-generational collective father-complexes yield over men.

Imagine Horatio having this chat with Hamlet. "Sire, you realize that your father was quite a nice king. But he wasn't perfect. Hamlet, my friend, it is truly evil that Claudius murdered him, usurped his throne, and is shacking up with your mother, but I implore you not to ruin your life with thoughts of revenge. Try to make the world better, not bloodier. So, go and marry Ophelia before she goes crazy and drowns herself in the river."

How do we persuade a man in the Middle East or Africa to make peace with his neighboring tribe and rebuke his culture's demand for a religious jihad against infidels? A man who projects his god-image onto a war-demanding deity will have none of it. A typical statement from either side goes something like this, "Yes, we want peace, but we cannot have peace when those evil infidels have killed our women and children." Hope for peace depends on whether men can reject duty to previous generations and grant themselves permission to move beyond their tribal complexes.

Collective-complexes can injure the psyche in other ways, such as taboos against marrying outside the ethnic family. Children from such cultures struggle whether to reject arranged marriages that place no value on the uniqueness of a child's Self. The collective cultural model that demands obedience causes children to suffer either guilt for rejecting the parental expectation or depression from foregoing the inner agenda of the Self.

Repetition of multi-generational traits that bring tragedy is called a family curse. The Kennedy family is an example of a family of men suffering several curses. One curse is the family expectation that Kennedy men become outspoken politicians who risk death. A less noble curse passed from Joe to his sons and grandsons is real men are womanizers. The tragic death at Chappaquiddick, the suicide of Marilyn Monroe, a rape in Florida, and a string of unhappy wives are the results of this family curse. A recent hopeful event for the Kennedy men is that Ted's son, Patrick, resigned from Congress after fourteen years. Patrick admits to wanting a different life than politics. Likely related is that he has struggled for years through substance addictions. Several months after his father died, finally Patrick was able to grant himself permission to pursue a more authentic life uninvolved in politics: a good outcome after much rehab and therapy, but delayed until his father's death.

Some men have a compensatory father-complex that drives them to be the opposite of their fathers. Disliking the negative traits of their fathers, they reject emulating their fathers. A father's alcoholism may induce the son to become a militant teetotaler. If the father has abused his mother the son may over-generalize that all men are abusive. If a son is ashamed of his father for being unemployed, criminal, or effeminate, he may become a workaholic, join the police force, or adopt a macho persona.

For example, FW had an alcoholic father who died and left his family penniless. FW devotes his life to abstinence and practices a righteous religious fundamentalism, but he is stifled, gruff, and has a sad countenance. He is unaware that his negative father-complex has abducted much potential joy and feeling from his life.

HF is a man of fifty-five. His father was selfish and abusive especially to HF's mother. HF compensates by idealizing his mother and women in general causing him to become a doormat for women at work and his wife at home. He also carries his mother's pain in his feminine shadow. He suffers because he cannot access the sense of manliness that is in his rejected father image.

CC's father owned a construction company. The father was a ruthless employer who mistreated his employees, including his sons. CC took over the business when his father retired. Unconsciously to compensate for his father's maltreatment, he gave excessive salaries to employees that bankrupted the company.

My father had many selfish habits. He would buy himself a two-pound can of peanuts and eat them without offering or sharing them with his children. Consequently I have an excessive need to give things away and share money with others, including an occasional scam artist.

Father-complex work involves separating the agenda of the individual's Self from the doctrine of his father while maintaining father's positive traits. As father-complex consciousness is obtained, a man often longs to reconnect with his father and relate to him as an adult friend.

Differentiating the agenda of our inner Self from that of our parents seems impossible when we have no conscious barometer of our true desire. The "the compass of desire," is a magical device in the movie, *"Pirates of the Caribbean"* that points to one's true desire. Comically the audience can intuit what the pirate desires despite his bravado of denial. A typical man in therapy lacks a compass of desire and cannot discriminate personal wishes from agenda items of his father introject.

> *The dreamer arrives in New York City by train. He struggles with his baggage and nearly loses a small important brown piece of luggage. An old man and a young boy want to share a cab with the dreamer. The old man appears derelict and run down. He wants to head west and the young boy wants to go east. The dreamer feels totally confused.*

New York City, the empire state's metropolis, is a symbol of vibrant opportunity for this man. This dream displays the status of his empire and his personal struggle. He is a typical mid-life man needing to overcome his decrepit father-complex. The old man is going west toward sunset (death) and the young vibrant lad is headed east toward the new day. The dreamer's confusion entails where to go and how to handle his (psychological) baggage. The important little bag that is nearly lost is his true desire.

Returning to Victor Frankenstein, his father problem is similar: will he handle his personal needs separately from his father introjects? Victor's middle brother, Earnest, is the first to awaken and greet him.

"Ah, I wish you had come three months ago, and then you would have found us all joyous and delighted."

(Chap 7, p. 29)

Victor's delay is cause to shudder. Three months is the length of a season. It is late August, the end of summer. Victor could have made the journey during May, but he dawdled the entire spring. Summer is a metaphor for Victor's mid-life. The junction of spring and summer in a man's psyche occurs sometime during his thirties when he can recover his soul before irreparable damage is done. Archetypes

137

remain accessible for transformation throughout a human's lifetime, but timing is important. When inner transformation is delayed, irrevocable harm may occur, as symbolized in Victor's complicity in William's death.

When a man brings in a dream that portends the imminent death of his anima or inner child, his analyst should drum into him the point that failure to make necessary changes imperils his soul. Victor's loss of his brother illustrates the consequences of failing to act expeditiously. We are all procrastinators. It is easy to be sympathetic to the analysand who is "trying" to remember his dreams and "intends" to do active imagination. However the analyst must clearly warn the analysand that the available time for inner transformative work is finite.

The Frankenstein family is intensely aggrieved. Father is heartbroken. Victor's brother, Edward, is barely consolable. Elizabeth is nearly catatonic with grief and worries about Justine.

Justine, the house-servant and quasi-adopted sister, has been falsely accused of committing William's murder. The golden locket with the image of Victor's mother was found in her clothing the night of the murder. The family and the police believe that stealing the golden locket was the motive for William's murder. Unbeknownst to her or the police, the monster planted the locket in her pocket to frame her.

The locket, a case hiding mother's face, represents Victor's mother-complex. Victor's wish to sustain his mother in life is responsible for the murder. The locket images how the mother-complex grabs us; her hidden image is like a collar that leads us to follow her agenda.

Justine is now the second casualty of Victor's unconscious mother-complex. The local authorities imprison Justine and set her trial for the exact day of Victor's return. Victor is aghast, knowing that his monster is the real culprit. He naively reassures Elizabeth that justice will prevail. One is naïve to believe that simply thinking nice thoughts will prevent the vengeful monster from causing tragedy.

NOTES FOR CHAPTER 7, Part 2, Father-Complex

1. There is a finite time to transform the shadow complexes before evil ensues.

Question: What father introjects do you need to confront?

2. We have triggers for re-activation of our complexes.

Question: How do family gatherings, telephone calls from home, or parental obligations make you feel?

3. The father-complex is a major force in shaping a man's life.

Questions: In what ways are you like your father? What do you secretly wish to experience that would elicit your father's disapproval?

4. Therapy requires deconstructing the influences of one's father in order to separate the agenda of one's Self from that of his father. Nearly every aspect of life is affected.

Question: How well does your compass-of-desire function?

5. The father-complex is a force in the unconscious that causes the influence of one's father to supersede the needs of one's Self.

Questions: How has your occupation been influenced by your father's opinion?

How is your treatment of women like your father's?

In what ways have you failed your father and felt ashamed?

How powerless do you feel powerless in the presence of your father or other men?

What do you dislike most about your father?

What in life makes you feel less than manly?

What tasks do you feel obligated to perform that cause irritation?

What areas are missing in your life feel because your father would not approve of them?

What curses exist for the men in your father's family or the men in your mother's family?

CHAPTER 8

Justine's name is a pun, a reversal of "injustice." On the day of William's murder she visited an aunt several miles away. When she returned to Geneva at nightfall a man informed her that the town was searching for William. She felt a duty to join the search, both as house-servant and quasi-sister to the boy. Beyond duty she genuinely loved the innocent child and searched late into the night. Exhausted, she bedded down in a horse stall after the city gates closed.

The innocent child and the innocent feminine are interrelated in a man's psyche. Men tease other men for displaying sensitivity by calling them girls or sissies. A man's ego responds to de-sissify himself by abandoning the child and feminine archetypes into the unconscious. Disassociating from the inner child and feminine allows a man to feel brave and manly; it also allows him to abuse others. The hyper-masculine persona unconsciously fears the sensitivity of the child and feminine because it threatens this false bravado. Thus the archetypes of inner child and feminine justice become psychic cell-mates within a man's shadow, typically solidifying during adolescence. Orphaning the divine child and young feminine into the unconscious impairs the ability of the adult man to care for others less powerful. A hyper-masculine man is more likely to exploit the weak than treat them with compassion.

> *The dreamer is in a car driving through a nice upscale*
> *residential area when he witnesses a crash in which a car gets*
> *broad-sided by a pick-up truck. The pick-up truck is clearly*
> *at fault. Its driver, a scruffy man, chases away the woman*
> *driver of the car and refuses to acknowledge his fault. The*
> *dreamer keeps quiet and is afraid of the situation. Next a*
> *policeman arrives and lies to the dreamer, proclaiming there*
> *was no accident. The dreamer is exasperated by this lie. The*
> *policeman transforms into an old man and then into the*
> *dreamer's father. The dreamer stuffs his father into a coffin-*
> *like refrigerator.*

The dream displays male injustice to the innocent woman, the essence of patriarchy. First, the truck smashes her car (a metaphor for ruining her life); next, the driver chases her away (overpowers her), then the policeman denies her property losses from the accident (devalues her rights and experience). The latter also means denying the feminine is no accident but a deliberate conspiracy in the psyche of the dreamer.

This dreamer's father-complex is represented by the policeman who treats the woman unjustly. The father is stuffed away and well preserved in the refrigerator, an apt symbol for the active presence of the father-complex. Similar to the violation of the feminine in this dream, Justine is deceived and railroaded by the police.

The morning after William's murder the police find Justine asleep in the barn straw. The local officials arrest her and accuse her of his murder in part because she is a young woman who had stayed out all night. Would the patriarchy vilify a man who stayed out all night? At trial Victor and Elizabeth spoke eloquently on behalf of Justine and the judges considered releasing her, but they hesitated because Justine could not account for William's locket in her coat pocket.

Victor and Elizabeth visit the police station the following day in hopes that Justine will be released. They discover that Justine has been found guilty, not by the circumstantial evidence, but by Justine's own confession! The betrothed couple listens in disbelief to Justine's confession:

"I did confess; but I confessed a lie. I confessed, that I

might obtain absolution; but now that falsehood lies heavier at my heart than all my other sins. The God of heaven forgive me!"

(Chap 8, par 22)

Following her arrest a patriarchal clergyman badgered Justine to make a confession. He threatened to ex-communicate her from the church if she refused, which would sentence her to hell. She reasoned if she accepted a death sentence with eternal life it was superior to a life with eternal damnation imposed by the Church. Effectively her confession was coerced using spiritual torture; and she was hanged.

This may seem inane by today's standards, but in the early eighteenth century the dogma of the church potentates was more potent. Catholics are still expected to believe the Pope is infallible. When Justine abdicates control of her soul to the local priest, it leads to her death. The moral: tragedy results when personal authenticity is abdicated to dogma. Metaphorically the archetype of inner feminine justice is sentenced to death when the feminine is treated unjustly by a dominant masculine authority.

What specifically is feminine justice? Acts include ensuring the wellbeing of children, feeding the hungry, and sheltering the homeless. A man who has lost contact with his feminine justice turns a cold eye to the helpless and disenfranchised. He is a businessman who operates factories in third world countries at a huge profit while paying laborers pennies per hour and polluting the environment. He is an executive who maintains a glass ceiling that denies women promotions. He is a military officer who sacrifices his own troops and slaughters civilians for non-human profit. Feminine justice is lacking in a society that justifies spending twenty percent of its GNP on a for-profit healthcare system that provides lavish corporate bonuses, while sixty million people go without health insurance. Lost contact with the feminine justice archetype is a pre-requisite to engaging in torture and espionage. Racism requires an absence of feminine justice. Political pundits and talk show hosts who shout down opponents have lost contact with their archetypal energies of feminine justice and respect.

Male chauvinism denigrates feminine processes by ridiculing

women's conversations, referring to them as cackling hens, and dismissing women's emotional reactions as evidence of weakness. Women's intuition is viewed by the patriarchy as stupidity when it fails, or as dumb luck when it succeeds.

The earth mother is an image of mature feminine justice. She cares about future generations and the environment. That businessman operating a factory in Mexico to avoid air pollution laws in the U.S. has sequestered his feminine justice function deep into his unconscious.

Vandalism by teenage boys is a common symptom of the repressed feminine sense of justice. Adolescent boys, surging with male hormones and machismo, can destroy property without remorse for the property owners' losses. A heinous form of this occurred several years ago. Angst-driven teenage boys engaged in a fad of finding skid-row derelicts, dousing them with gasoline, and burning them to death.

Sadly our social institutions often contribute to the alienation of young men from their sense of feminine justice. The judicial and penal systems imprison young men where they are subjected to sadistic cruelty from other inmates and prison guards. Most prisons and many schools teach young men, implicitly through harsh rules and insensitive treatment, that power and submission rule the world rather than human justice.

A man's readiness for transformation to regain contact with his inner child and social justice function is subtle and easily missed. An analysand whose unconscious is attempting to re-establish a consciousness of feminine justice and the inner child may dream of suffering children or waifs. Other men whose psyches are attempting to compensate may send them dream images of collective suffering, such as famines or indiscriminate killing. Disintegrating masculine structures like the military or factories are also dream motifs of the need to soften the masculine with a balancing feminine aspect. The following dream illustrates the complacency of the prevailing culture amid dangers to the collective feminine. The factory is a dream image of the entrenched patriarchal hierarchy.

The dreamer is on the shores of the ocean. Turning inland he notices a storm brewing over a General Motors factory.

There are men urging the dreamer to buy more GM stock. The dreamer is trying to convince the people that lightning is striking the plant, but the crowd will not listen. The factory catches fire and only the dreamer seems to notice. Women in the path of the expanding flames are injured. The dreamer runs away.

This dream illustrates the dreamer's emerging consciousness (seashore) that cautions him to ignore the cultural patriarchy's push to "buy more stock" in the old factory. The dream is attempting to make the dreamer conscious of the imminent danger to his feminine that the factory symbolizes.

Justine failed to defend herself against the doctrine of her church. Victor also failed to speak timely on her behalf. Despite Justine's death sentence, Victor chose to protect his ego and could not bring himself to confess the creation of the monster. The innocent feminine suffers the injury of the unconscious patriarchal monster. Justine's death from Victor's dawdling to claim his monster responsibilities can serve as another warning to analysands to attend to their shadow work in a timely manner.

> **"And on the morrow Justine died…My passionate and indignant appeals were lost upon them. And when I received their cold answers, and heard the harsh unfeeling reasoning of these men, my purposed avowal died away on my lips."**
>
> **(Chap 8, par 31)**

Silent complicity is the glue that holds together many systems of injustice: patriarchy, Nazism, racism, genocide, etc. Each requires a silent and complicit citizenry to flourish. Although Victor did try to convince the police of her innocence, he hid the existence of the monster. The often-quoted line of Edmund Burke applies, "All that is necessary for evil to prevail is for good men to do nothing."

The dreamer is on a boat at sea. He spies a woman bobbing in the water near the shore. He shouts that she is drowning, but no one seems concerned. Next he listens to the captain who instructs him on how to navigate 40 foot waves from the wakes of ocean liners. He is terrified.

In another dream:

The dreamer is dining with two women present. He notices their hands are red and transplanted onto their arms. He asks the women if their nerves have feelings.

These dream images convey that the inner feminine is being mistreated by the ego. In the first the feminine is in danger of downing. The dreamer's challenge is how to maneuver the mechanical boat captained by the old guard. Forty-foot waves produced by the ocean liners certainly would drown a woman in the ocean. This represents how monumental a task it is to overcome the power of the patriarchy. In the second dream the feminine hands are cut off. There are numerous tales of handless maidens. These tales convey feminine impotence in our culture. Notice the man wonders if their nerves (ability to feel) have any residual function. The dreamer is one who has lost his ability to feel.

Cold, unfeeling, harsh, and principled are adjectives for men whose feminine justice archetype is abandoned to the shadow. They describe men who provoke innocent death in the world. Each Hitler, Attila, Hussein, Pol Pot, and serial killer of the world has a dead Justine inside.

NOTES FOR CHAPTER 8

1. The archetype of the innocent child is associated in the psyche with that of feminine justice. Each has a loving nature toward others and values fairness.

Question: Does feeling joyful like a child or responding with sensitivity make you feel unmanly?

2. Feminine justice regulates our capacity for charity, kindness, and inclusiveness.

Question: For what groups of people does sympathizing seem most difficult for you?

3. The unconscious suppression of justice may manifest as dream images of distressed children or collective casualties, particularly of injured women.

Question: Can you recall any dream images of children or women in danger?

CHAPTER 9

Haunted by the deaths, Victor is past denial of his monster. He knows not what to do; therefore, he lapses into despair. He contemplates suicide:

> "I left my boat to pursue its own course, and gave way to my own miserable reflections. I was often tempted...to plunge into the silent lake, that the waters might close over me and my calamities for ever."

>   (Chap 9, par 5)

The grief that accompanies confronting one's shadow is frequently accompanied by suicidal thoughts. Powerlessness compels the ego to contemplate suicide as a means to maintain control. Like Hitler at the end of WWII, the ego would rather die than submit to the control of another. Suicide is a persistent threat to the analysand who resists "letting go."

Suicides peak during the transitions of adolescence, midlife, and old age. The mid-life peak transition is especially hazardous due to three overwhelming insults to the ego: the fear of growing old, the discovery of one's shadow, and the absence of hope for the future. Suicide might be contemplated by a brash stockbroker who is being investigated by the SEC or a basketball star arrested for sexual assault as face-losing events expose the shadow and ruin the persona. Victor rues that his ego cannot rectify the murders or reconcile his monster problem. He becomes hopeless.

> **"Elizabeth was sad and desponding; she no longer took delight in her ordinary occupations…She was no longer that happy creature…who in earlier youth wandered with me… and talked with ecstasy of our future prospects."**
>
> **(Chap 9, par 7)**

As Victor lacks hope, so does Elizabeth, his anima projection, who expresses his despair along with hers. Although a depressed person cannot envision a solution to his despair, there is always hope, as the Self will struggle for survival using dreams, synchronicity, or impulsive actions in its drive for completion. Victor's Self sends him an impulse to walk in the mountains.

> **"…but sometimes the whirlwind passion of my soul drove me to seek, by bodily exercise and by change of place, some relief from intolerable sensations. It was during an access of this kind that I suddenly left my home, and bending my steps towards the near Alpine valleys, sought in the magnificence, the eternity of such scenes, to forget myself and my ephemeral, because human, sorrows."**
>
> *(Chap 9, par 12)*

Victor impulsively leaves Geneva to retreat in the mountain woods for reflection. He is inexplicably called from within to hike up to the mountain village of Chamonix, a favorite boyhood stop. Chamonix is an Alpine valley whose name means the seeds of the earth, metaphorically a place where the inner soul has the potential to germinate into a fruitful life.

It is noteworthy that a component of the inner child archetype has arranged for Victor to re-visit a favorite town of his childhood, and his inferior sensate function sends him some joy from the scenery. The Alps, the Swiss' Olympus, indicates Victor's Self has sent him to land of the gods. Our tone-deaf-to-spirit modernity scoffs at such inner callings. In Charles Dickens's *A Christmas Carol* Scrooge dismisses the apparition of Jacob Marley as a case of indigestion.

Victor hikes into the mountains unknowing that his Self has arranged a confrontation with his monster. A man in therapy may have dreams in which monster figures appear. The terror of confronting the monster may be overcome and transformed through active imagination dialogues. It is time for Victor to dialogue with his monster.

NOTES FOR CHAPTER 9

1. There comes a time when we can no longer deny our shadow. Denial becomes perilous when the ego feels hopeless and shameful.

Question: When did you first know you had an inexorable monster?

2. The ego may consider suicide as a solution. The stronger one's ego convictions and the weaker one's trust in the mystery and hope of inner process, the greater the likelihood that an actual suicide will occur.

Question: When you identified your monster, did you run? Did you consider suicide? Did you confess your sins to another?

3. The Self will draw attention to shadow contents with dreams and synchronistic associations. The unconscious becomes the spring soil offering a new psychic life.

Question: Have you experienced dream images of monsters begging for attention?

CHAPTER 10

Victor's Self lures the protagonist to into the Chamonix Mountains on a pretext of pleasure. Despite an overnight stay in the village Victor awakens to his unchanged gloomy state, but the healing aspect of his psyche breaks though when he ascends a nearby glacier. In the natural splendor Victor experiences an epiphany, a feeling of divine presence, as he senses the spirit of nature.

> **"My heart which was before sorrowful, now swelled with something like joy; I exclaimed—'Wandering spirits, if indeed ye wander, and do not rest in your narrow beds, allow me this faint happiness, or take me, as your companion, away from the joys of life."**
>
> **(Chap 10, par 4)**

Victor's prayer is ambivalent. Not unusual for a depressed person, he wishes the gods to help him and doesn't particularly care if they heal him or kill him. Summoning the gods is serious business not to be undertaken lightly. "Be careful what you ask for; you may receive it!" Wham! As soon as Victor addresses the spirit world, the monster arrives leaping over glacial crevices like a gorilla bounding through a forest. Simultaneously it begins to rain, a metaphor for the outpouring of unconscious contents.

Mountains are the high thrones of the gods. A meeting in the mountains is a confrontation with the Self. Moses ascends a mountain when he receives stone tablets from God. Mountain dreams often portend a contact from the collective god-image or the personal god-image, the Self.

> The dreamer is in the mountains with a group of people including children. The people on the mountain top are aliens. There is a nice-looking man who the dreamer realizes has an agenda to take over control. The dreamer tries to stab the man but finds him invincible.

The aliens atop the mountain are archetypal characters of the collective unconscious. The dreamer feels the challenge to his ego's control and tries to stab the man, but he discovers the cold truth about the invincibility of the mountain aliens. Victor is having a similar mountain encounter with his invincible monster.

The monster is eager to dialogue with Victor. Active imagination requires a soft but firm meditative dialogue with an inner personification. Inactive imagination we do involuntarily at night in our dreams that are controlled by the dream-maker of the Self. In active imagination one uses the ego to summon up a character and then actively engages in a give-and-take dialogue. An excellent guide to this process is available in Robert Johnson's classic text, *Inner Work*.

Johnson's method has worked well for me. The process begins by closing your eyes and asking for a dream character to come forward. The ego then asks questions, responds, and negotiates with the character. The purpose is to learn as much as possible about what portion of the Self the character represents. Often the character will tell the analysand his name, as did my character, Tim. As the ego and Self are attempting to transcend their impasse and reach a mutually acceptable plan for the future, it is useful to write down the dialogue for later study. Do this immediately without reflection. Stay in the present moment of the dialogue. The ego should be humble and respectful. Victor starts off poorly by being disrespectful and arrogant.

> "Devil, do you dare approach me? And do you not fear the fierce vengeance of my arm wreaked on your miserable head? Begone, vile insect…"

(Chap 10, par 6)

To which the monster replies,

> "I expected this reception…All men hate the wretched; how, then must I be hated, who am miserable beyond all living things! Yet you, my creator, detest and spurn me, thy creature, to whom thou art bound by ties only dissoluble by the annihilation of one of us…Do your duty toward me, and I will do mine towards you and the rest of mankind. If you will comply with my conditions, I will leave them and you at peace; but if you refuse, I will glut the maw of death, until it be satiated with the blood of your remaining friends."

(Chap 10, par 7)

This is the Full Monty! The monster has laid out the conditions of their relationship in his first speech with crystal clarity. He demands that Victor engage in mutual assistance or annihilation. The promise of successful monster work is peace and tranquility for Victor and his loved ones. The drama of the second half of the book is whether Victor can successfully negotiate a solution to his monster problem.

The power of active imagination is proven when we receive such blunt wisdom and direction from our monster as has Victor. This ritual of deep personal work and communication is more than just a "leap of faith." There is ample empirical data to substantiate the value of active imagination.

Jung believed the Self makes an honest attempt to be clear. Sometimes the characters of active imagination and dreams speak directly as does Victor's monster, but other times the Self's language is encoded in images or words that the ego cannot understand. A therapist skilled in the translation of symbolic psychic discourse

155

is often required because our ego tends to blindly resist an obvious message. I am typical. I am skilled at dream interpretation, but I must regularly call analyst friends to decode my dream images.

The following is a personal example of monster dialogue. I had a dream of being frightened by a vampire in the basement of the farmhouse of my childhood. I summoned the vampire for a conversation.

Greg: *Who are you, vampire? I can remember your face from my dream. Can we talk? Go ahead and bite my neck. I'll go with you for now. Why do you suck the blood out of me?*

(Compare my greeting and invitation to Victor's "Devil...begone.")

Vampire: It is our blood.

(The monster told Victor that they were *"bound by ties only dissoluble by annihilation of one of us."*)

Greg: *You mean I am you? Sharing my blood with dark parts of me?*
Vampire: *Ha, ha, ha, ha, ha,...(condescendingly)*
Greg: *I can't allow you to run my life. I need my spirit to do good.*
Vampire: *Go away!*
Greg: *No, I want to deal with you. Get this out in the open.*
Vampire: *Why have you neglected us?*
Greg: *How?*
Vampire: *By pushing us down in the basement since you were seven.*

(The basement is a synonym for the shadow realm.)

Greg: *What happened when we were seven?*
Vampire: *The windows you broke with the baseballs house caused you guilt and pain.*

(I had an unlucky penchant for breaking windows with baseballs. This angered my father, not inappropriately, but I came to associate play with shame and it became an aspect of my vampire, my shadow creature of desire.)

Greg: *When I played baseball, it was fantasy to escape my home life.*

Vampire: *The upper world escaped; the lower world got trapped.*

(The vampire lives in the lower world.)

Greg: *How can we re-unite them?*
Vampire: *I want to live again. I want to walk on the earth.*
Greg: *Fine, how can I help?*
Vampire: *Open the door to the basement.*
Greg: *How? I see you spraying blood back from your fangs into my mouth. I don't get it.*
Vampire: *I am purging myself.*
Greg: *What does the blood mean?*
Vampire: *Spirit of unlived potentials.*
Greg: *Such as?*
Vampire: *The force of light in the chest.*

(He is pointing to my body's chest.)

Greg: *How can I unblock it?*
Vampire: *The deep pain of the early years is what grows the vampires down here in the basement like mushrooms in the dark.*
Greg: *How does that get healed?*
Vampire: *Drink the blood here!*

(He shoots more blood from his fangs into my mouth. Drinking blood is an image of healing transformation. Drinking the blood of Jesus enables spiritual healing in Christian iconography.)

Greg: *Drinking blood makes one a vampire, but it also has a Eucharistic aspect. How can a vampire do that?*
Vampire: *We are the union of life and death. It cycles.*
Greg: *Will I get your energy back? I wish I could see you walk out of the basement.*
Vampire: *We avoid the light.*
Greg: *Are you permanently fixed in the dark? Are you unable to walk out of the light and join me in the upper world?*
Vampire: *I don't know.*
Greg: *Come try to walk with me in the light. I won't change your being. In the stories of vampires they are immortal except for the wood stake through the heart. Would you like a stake in the heart to be reborn?*
Vampire: *It's too terrifying.*

(Notice the change in tone of the vampire from vicious to vulnerable fear. Remember he formed when I was seven. This activity requires ego development. As a child and young adult I was too immature and afraid of vampires to do this work.)

Greg: *I see. But it is terrifying for me to have you haunt me in my dreams. Let's both die and be reborn. Kneel down and I'll pound this stake into your heart.*

(*I scream for myself and the vampire as I imagine this act. I feel nauseous. My arms are weak. I cry. I carry the vampire up onto the driveway and lay him in the sun. A cloud appears to shade him. I hug him. I look into the basement and the other vampires have gone. The sun comes out. I give thanks to the heavens. I vow to tear down the house and expose the basement to the sunlight to heal, not destroy, the vampires.*)

Greg: *Vampire, are you there, inside me now? No longer afraid of the light?*
Vampire: *I still walk here in the shadow, but I do not fear.*
Greg: *Are you a death wish? For me or for others?*

(My suicidal fears?)

Vampire: *I am the spirit of revenge which when activated is a death sentence on your spirit.*
Greg: *How can I keep you from operating?*
Vampire: *Just knowing I'm here is enough to help.*
Greg: *I hope you'll go easy on me.*
Vampire: *I'll take smaller bites.*

Two decades later this active imagination is still powerful to me. I am struck by the transformation of the vampire. The vampire remains in my shadow but is calmer when I am simply aware of him. During the active imagination I visualized him coming into the light, i.e., gaining awareness of the presence of my vampiric potential. But the vampire says he is hesitant to come out of the basement, hence shadow contents can exist hidden in a comfort zone. I am awed by the appearance of the cloud as it arises to shield the vampire from direct sun. Images of humans conversing with God often contain clouds that buffer the humans from direct viewing of the sun/god.

My experience includes several typical aspects of active imagination with the inner monster. The dialogue is accompanied by terror, gooseflesh, and shaking knees. The engagement contains images and physical movement. My greatest fear is always the unknown. Even after twenty years I am still not sure what all the statements by the vampire mean. But I clearly understand that childhood pain is connected with the vampire's capacity for vengeance. I am aware now that when I feel vengeful, I should look for a childhood origin.

Discourse with the monster is scary and requires ego strength. Will the monster take over and turn me into a sociopath? Will he make me suicidal? Will the monster tell me something really unbearable about myself or request something completely unacceptable to my ego? The analyst is responsible for evaluating an analysand's ego strength and preparing him for engagement with the unconscious.

My vampire warns me that he is ready to perpetrate vengeance if I fail to express certain playful aspects of my Self. Revenge is the central theme of *Hamlet*. Reaching a satisfactory balance between the ego and the Self is difficult work. Failure is ominous; it resulted in madness and death for Hamlet.

Victor commits the error of rebuking the monster. The monster remains patient despite Victor's rudeness. An analyst would encourage Victor to listen to his monster, and consider that Victor's anger and rudeness is likely his fear of the monster. This encouragement may require multiple sessions to strengthen Victor's ego enough to tolerate remaining present with his monster.

Victor's monster, aware of his horrible potential, is not surprised that Victor hates him and listens quietly as Victor threatens to murder him. The Self knows the ego is a tough nut to crack. Victor refuses to accept responsibility for creating the monster and does not hear the annihilating consequences of abandoning him.

Suicide is not an option for the monster; but is available to his mortal creator. The monster, an archetype like my vampire, cannot die; it strives to express its libido. The monster instructs Victor with the conditions for assimilation. Do your duty towards me and you and mankind can go in peace. But you screw with me and I will destroy the relationships of importance to you! This is a non-negotiable stick-up: *your spiritual life or a blood bath!*

The personal work that is required of a man who is called toward wholeness can be excruciating. Edward Edinger's book, *The Christian Archetype*, explains that the suffering and crucifixion of Jesus parallels the horrific pain the ego experiences in yielding control to the Self. Jesus must acquiesce to God's plan; the ego must accept the agenda of the Self to individuate.

Tragically Victor has no intention of acquiescing to the monster's request for a relationship. He tries assaulting the monster physically. The monster dodges him easily and speaks to Victor in a calm voice.

> "Be calm, I entreat you to hear me, before you give vent to your hatred on my devoted head. Have I not suffered enough that you seek to increase my misery? Life, although it may only be an accumulation of anguish, is dear to me, and I will defend it. Remember, thou hast made me more powerful than thyself; my height is superior to thine, my joints more supple. But I will not be tempted to set myself in opposition to thee. I am thy creature, and I will be even mild and docile to my natural lord and king, if thou wilt also perform thy part, that which thou owest me. Oh, Frankenstein, be not equitable to every other, and trample upon me alone, to whom thy justice, and even thy clemency and affection is most due. Remember, that I am thy creature; I ought to be thy Adam; but I am rather the fallen angel, whom thou drivest from joy for no misdeed. Everywhere I see bliss, from which I alone am irrevocably excluded. I was benevolent and good; misery made me a fiend. Make me happy, and I shall again be virtuous."
>
> (Chap 10, par 10)

Victor's monster is remarkably patient with repeated pleas for Victor's ear and friendship, promising peace in return. It may appear paradoxical that the murdering monster says that life is dear and he wants to protect it. The monster's reference to life means his relationship with Victor and the monster's expression of his libido. If the latter requires committing outer murders to preserve Victor's shadow libido, so be it. Archetypes are not concerned with physical life and death.

Traditional Jewish, Christian, and Muslim monotheisms posit the existence of an outer God, and they prescribe rules that humans must follow in God's service without deference to themselves. In reward these monotheisms promise redemption in an afterlife. Humans have no value other than service to the outer God; their earthly life is inconsequential.

Depth psychology values and honors the individual human Self intrinsically without reference to an outer deity. The Self must have no gods before it, specifically the ego or any Self co-opting construct. Discharging the agenda of the Self demands the ego integrates the psychic components of the Self, particularly the shadow-monster and the anima spirit. Failure means to live in misery, a metaphoric Hell. Thus a basic rift exists between depth psychology and religion: which is the god that must be obeyed?

Does that mean we can all do as we please? Can a serial killer murder at will? Not at all! Consider Dennis Rader, the BTK serial killer. BTK is his self-named acronym for bind, torture, and kill. Bound in the shadow and given no outlet of expression, the monster feels tortured and killed. Dennis Rader revenges these three feelings via his ritual pattern of BTK. Listening to his gruesome story of slowly strangling a nine-year-old girl with tools from his "hit kit" confirms he has no contact with his inner Justine that carries his empathy.

The majority of us do have Selfs with an inherent social connection, a collective spirit, that drives our cooperation with and contribution to others. Carl Jung and Edward Edinger each spent their final years writing about the evolving transformation of the god-image that will value individuation. It differs from the schema of current religions that control human behavior on earth by promising either a reward in heaven or punishment in hell. The evolving god-image values individuation as an asset of the collective good.

My speculation is that the eventual new god-image will revere the planet as a sacred ecological home to all life. Preserving nature's balance to allow humans and other creatures to live out their potentials will become a collective value. As a result human psychological wholeness will be valued, particularly as the individual supports the collective viability of the planet. A recent popular film, *Avatar*, is an artistic expression of an evolving reverence for ecological balance.

The monster's pleas are a guidebook for transforming monster potentials. Individuation, the integration of the unconscious, is a task of Self-love implying the ego becomes reverently subordinate to the Self. In 12-Step jargon this is letting go to a higher power. One difficulty is accepting that the Self contains the shadow which is akin to accepting that Satan is an aspect of God. The West has split good and evil into God and Satan with the latter commanding the shadow. Christianity has cast humans as carriers of sin. The orthodox churches do not support individuation, i.e. valuing our totality including its "sinful" aspects. The Frankenstein monster compares his treatment by Victor to God's rejection of Satan from heaven. The monster pleads with Victor to treat him as a son like Adam, not to avoid him as evil like Satan.

Victor refuses. Resisting integration of the shadow means the soul is cut-off; for the collective it means crimes of vengeance. Keep BTK in mind. Sadly society follows the same path as Victor. When it rejects the psychic monster and refuses to dialogue and transform its monster potentials, devastation is invited. The death penalty fails to prevent murder. No-tolerance school policies increase teen acting out gun violence. Criminalization of drugs out of fear of addiction creates prison-hardened felons rather than a drug-free society. The Holocaust museum in Washington, D.C. displays the results of one incident of genocide but prohibits discussing the psychological causes of genocide. Refusing to explore the causes for hatred and genocide in the collective shadow contributes to the failure to prevent genocides subsequent to the Holocaust such as have occurred in Rwanda, Darfur, Serbia, Iraq, and Somalia.

The monster persists in his attempts to convince Victor to accept him.

> **"How can I move thee? Will no entreaties cause thee to turn a favourable eye upon thy creature who implores thy goodness and compassion?"**

> **(Chap 10, par 12)**

And,

> **"Listen to my tale: when you have heard that, abandon or commiserate me, as you shall judge that I deserve. But hear me."**
>
> **(Chap 10, par 12)**

Victor is indignant and irritated that he should endure listening to this awful creature, as might a fundamentalist Christian who is asked to have tea and a chit-chat with Satan!

> **"Why do you call to my remembrance, circumstances, of which I shudder to reflect, that I have been the miserable origin and author? Cursed be the day, abhorred devil, in which you first saw light!"**
>
> **(Chap 10, par 13)**

The glacial landscape where the monster lives is equivalent to the barren inner landscape of Victor's soul. The icy cold is a universal image for being out of touch with one's feelings. The tough ice-man persona connotes dismissal of feelings. Like a double-agent spy, an unemotional man lives a double life; his outer tough guy persona is cold and stiff while his inner is alive with emotion. Relating to the unconscious requires the ego persona to "come in from the cold."

> *The dreamer is a teenage boy stuck in a steel conduit like a storm sewer pipe. He feels the need to break the walls and escape. As the dreamer begins to separate the walls he encounters layer upon layer of steel and cement. At last the pipe wall is opened to the sky and he escapes.*

Being stuck is an inherent part of the psychotherapeutic journey. It is cold and frustrating like Victor's encounter with the monster. Engaging the Self in dialogue and submitting to the demands of the unconscious is an uphill grind of dissolving ego resistance. Pointing out dream images that indicate "stuck-ness" helps the analysand overcome his impasse. Stuckness is so common it often consumes large parts of therapeutic sessions.

Victor's stuck-ness is loosened by his scientific curiosity. Victor begrudgingly agrees to hear to the monster's tale when the monster reminds Victor that he bears a responsibility for his creation. Victor's curiosity draws him to visit the monster's hut on the glacier. His dominant thinking function motivates him to follow the monster into the ice cave to hear his story. Often an analyst can engage an analysand via the seduction of his superior function. Victor does not comprehend or believe that benevolence and compassion are the benefits of befriending the monster, but his willingness to listen conveys hope.

NOTES FOR CHAPTER 10

1. Your Self will alert your ego that to the work that is necessary through images in dreams, synchronistic events, and obsessive tugging for your attention.

Question: What specific events have brought you to a crisis or into therapy?

2. The spirits will answer when called. Be prepared.

Question: Can you endure the knee-knocking fear of hearing your true nature and faults?

3. Active imagination is a useful tool to converse with shadow figures. Listen specifically for the causes of the monster's pain and why he is hiding. These are areas that require healing and are potential sources of retribution by the monster if neglected.

Question: What vengeful acts have you done that you can ask your monster about?

4. Embracing the totality of the Self is a life-engaging practice. It will likely require that religious dogma be replaced by a personal willingness to serve your Self.

Question: Do you have a religious objection to admitting the monster side of yourself is part of an internal god-image, the Self?

5. Stuck-ness is an omnipresent condition of ego resistance. Expect it, look for it, and fight it.

Question: Can you identify fears or restrictions that keep you from confronting your shadow characters?

CHAPTER 11

The exiled monster tells his story sitting near the door of his glacial cave. The cave entrance is metaphorically the door to Victor's monster work. This and the next four chapters convey the monster's whereabouts from the time Victor created him to their current meeting on the glacier. The monster's autobiography explains how he found food, became educated, and struggled to fulfill his needs of acceptance and relationship.

After the monster ran away from Victor's Ingolstadt lab, he quickly learned to hide deep in the woods because his initial encounters with humans brought rejection. People reacted to the monster with screams of terror and beat him. Early in his life the monster is incapable of speech and ignorant of everything. He is toddler-like with mobility, but lacks language or understanding. The monster is relegated to his hidden refuge, as was my Trench-Coat Man who became basement-bound in my dreams at age two.

The people who interact with the monster are his symbolic parents and culture who display horror at his presence and condemn his acts. They naively believe they have successfully expunged this dangerous and ugly part of the natural child, but the monster lives. It is appropriate and necessary for socialization that the child's primitive animal be corralled. The terrible twos are exasperating for parents, but it is more painful for the toddler who loses conscious contact with a natural part of his individuality. Robert Bly's classic, *Iron John*, describes the forest shadow creature of instinct that grows from toddler to adult in a man's unconscious.

Victor's monster awakens to bright sunshine on his second day, but he again is shamed upon entering a house in the woods. The occupant screams and runs away, impelling the monster to flee deeper into the forest.

The monster tells Victor about his delight in discovering his primitive senses.

> **"…a stronger light pressed upon my nerves, so I was obliged to shut my eyes; ….but hardly had I felt this, when by opening my eyes, as I now suppose, the light poured in upon me again."**
>
> **(Chap 11, par 1)**

> **"The light became more and more oppressive to me, and, the heat wearying me as I walked, I sought a place where I could receive shade."**
>
> **(Chap 11, par 1)**

The daylight, although delightful, is painful to the monster's new eyes. This is a metaphor for the monster's suffering when exposed or brought to light, i.e., being seen. The sensations and feelings of the monster must be kept in darkness. The greater the shame, the deeper the monster must hide. The monster scurries into the next village and is met with more horror; children scream. This particularly saddens the monster who wishes to play with children.

Peer pressure exacerbates monster vengeance during adolescence. The Columbine teens committed their murders in retaliation for being teased. They purposely bypassed killing several female classmates whom they encountered during the massacre because the girls had treated them nicely. The Columbine massacre wasn't merely an indiscriminant psychotic killing spree; it was planned vengeance by monsters; and shows that accepting one's monster curbs its violent potential.

Townspeople hurl stones at Victor's monster and strike him with sticks. This violent teasing, besides making him retreat deeper into the forest, enhances his rage at humans who reject him.

A dreamer is in a restaurant-theater in a public space. A man is murdered by an acquaintance of the dreamer who asks that the dreamer to assist him in hiding the body and removing evidence of the murder. The dreamer removes incriminating fibers and places misleading items of false evidence at the scene. The dreamer feels guilty over his part of the cover-up. He notices an attic door and pulls some old linen sheets out and wonders what they mean.

In dreams, murders of unknown men for unknown reasons are images of shadow creation. The acquaintance of the above dreamer represents the dreamer's ego-persona that created his shadow. The attic is a storage place and sheets are materials used to cover up attic artifacts. This dream is pushing the dreamer to "uncover" the dead man, i.e., to revive his shadow libido.

A common setting in dreams and fairy tales, the forest represents the place where shadow energies reside. The Frankenstein monster retreats into the woods to hide. Similarly our intolerable attributes hide in our shadows. Shadow elements look for opportunities of expression. Unconscious habits, compulsions, and periods of depression are expressions of subsisting shadow elements. Addiction specialists know that eliminating alcohol will only cause a new addiction to take its place. The addictive process is a release valve for libido trapped in the unconscious and searching for expression.

An omnipresent danger from the shadow-monster-in-hiding is his proclivity to jump out at the worst possible time: when we are angry. When a man is arguing with his wife and his emotional lava flow nears the surface, the monster is waiting for an opportunity to jump out and become violent. A wall is punched, or worse, the wife is battered.

Although winter snow covered the woods the monster lives easily. He explains to Victor that he has super-human traits that allow him to suffer extremes of cold and heat that mortal humans cannot. The metaphor is that you cannot kill the monster by simply relegating him to the cold shadows.

One day while wandering in the woods, the Frankenstein monster discovers a farm with an empty lean-to enclosure within a pigsty that is hidden from the house. The monster covers up the entry and sides of the lean-to so that:

"All the light I enjoyed came through the sty, and that was sufficient for me."

(Chap 11, par 12)

Prior to accepting our shadows only an occasional faint light of awareness illuminates our pigsties, i.e., the times when we are being little pigs. Being a pig is a moment of dirtiness, perhaps gluttony, lascivious acts, or bold rudeness. A favorite activity of men is raucous drinking which gives an outlet for pigginess such as weekend frat parties in college. The boys-nights-out of gambling, drinking, viewing pornography, and visiting strip clubs are recurring shadow outlets for many men. Ancient traditions celebrated the festivals of Bacchus and Pan, drunken and lewd orgiastic events. Modern festivals include Halloween, Carnivale, Mardi Gras, and "What happens in Vegas, stays in Vegas" to "give the devil his due." While letting loose helps vent the pressure in the shadow's volcano, a more conscious integration of shadow contents will ultimately produce a more satisfying life experience.

Victor's monster continues his biography from chapter eleven through sixteen, a long exposition. Shelley's literary purpose is to augment the metaphors with parallel characters with struggles similar to those of Victor and the monster, but having redeeming attributes that Victor lacks.

From within his pigsty the monster watches a family that inhabits the farm: a daughter named Agatha, her brother Felix, and their father. Through eavesdropping, the monster learns that the family was previously of aristocratic Russian nobility. Agatha is sad and frustrated. Felix wishes he could help his father and sister. The family is exiled from France, living in poverty; the monster is exiled from Victor, living in a pigsty.

Agatha means "good," representing the good feminine and feeling side of the anima. Victor has lost a personal connection with his feeling function and projects this part of himself on his mother and Elizabeth. Felix, from the Latin "filus," means son, the young masculine. He longs for relationship, particularly with a woman. He represents the state of Victor's the lost boyhood and unmet desires that make him depressed.

Shadow work can over-emphasize one's dark side and neglect positive shadow elements. Agatha and Felix represent positive traits within Victor's shadow. Agatha loves the music her father plays, representing Victor's sensate aspect. Felix, a passionate man who cannot wait to marry Safie, the woman he loves, is the opposite of Victor's ego persona that values work and study over romantic love. My own positive shadow contained creative abilities of writing that my father pooh-poohed as valueless. Other positive qualities of my shadow were an interest in music, assertiveness, and a feminine quality of nurturing.

It may seem counter-intuitive that the shadow has positive attributes that are difficult for a man to access. Why wouldn't a man want to be sociable, outgoing, and creative? Accessing shadow contents, whether negative or positive, makes us uncomfortable. It feels awkward, guilty, or immoral. First, the ego doesn't value the qualities as positive and his persona denies the traits. Second, an external source of shame has pushed the positive qualities into the shadow. Third, the ego feels guilt and fear towards the positive shadow traits because they lie in proximity to the evil aspects of one's shadow. For example, I feel guilty that writing is feminine (sissy and non-masculine) and a waste of time (an activity of sloth). My creative urges reside in my shadow alongside my potential for sloth and softness. Help to access a positive shadow trait can occur if an analysand admires the trait in another man thus allowing it to take root to grow in his own consciousness.

The father of the exiled family, Mr. DeLacy, represents the positive father-complex component of Victor. Blind Mr. DeLacy is kind and musical which is unlike Victor's father who sees black and white and shuns the artistic for the practical.

Each day Felix is exhausted from collecting and chopping wood for fuel. The life of the family is imperiled by a dwindling supply of firewood. The monster notices. He falls in love with the family. The monster carries the ability to love and care for family that Victor has lost to his work compulsion.

The countenance of the old man captures the heart of the monster. His face conveys the acceptance and affection that the monster desires. One day when the father is alone, the monster visits him. The blind man enjoys the delightful companionship of the monster, unlike those who only see his exterior and run in revulsion. The idealized father will look at his child with a beaming approval. A son can see in his father's eyes a message of pleasure or disgust. What the monster craves is approval, not the evil-eye of those who reject him, especially Victor's.

When Agatha breaks down sobbing from the pain of living in poverty, her father gently comforts her. The compassion displayed from father to daughter induces in the monster:

"...a mixture of pain and pleasure, such as I had never before experienced...I withdrew from the window, unable to bear these emotions."

(Chap 11. par 15)

One finds unbearable the expression of the pain trapped in the shadow. The dog-eat-dog world of commercial competition disparages feelings in men. Compassionate feelings are dangerous to the economic and political structures. Agents of business demand loyalty because allowing workers to experience sensitivity interferes with production, inhibits exploitation, and reduces profitability.

The following dream came to a man in therapy who was unaware of the extent of intra-psychic abuse he suffered from his patriarchal loyalty.

The dreamer is a man being trained as a team member of a football team. The training involves a ritual of a large bulky player raping the dreamer via anal intercourse. The dreamer and the other players then ritually stab themselves in their hearts.

Stabbing oneself in the heart is a loss of the feeling function. The loss is necessary to accept abuse by the patriarchy symbolized by the sodomy. That is the state of Victor's feeling function as experienced in the monster: lost and abused.

NOTES FOR CHAPTER 11

1. The goal of shadow work is to find an outlet for its libido.

Question: Can you name two fantasy desires that you consider evil or bad?

2. Positive shadow qualities exist that also need accession and expression.

Question: Can you name two fantasy desires that are socially acceptable but you are inexplicably incapable of achieving?

3. Valuing shadow contents is difficult.

Question: What is it about the negative qualities above that makes you uncomfortable when you imagine displaying those traits?

4. Accessing shadow contents is assisted by finding similar qualities in other men and developing an appreciation for the quality.

Question: Can you name men who exhibit traits listed above that you admire and despise? For those men you admire, envision yourself expressing their traits. For those you despise, identify how can you discharge the libido represented by their despicable traits?

5. The moments of shadow breakthrough are often heralded by seeing the pain of your shadow in another.

Question: What emotional expression do you find unbearable to watch? Can you remember feeling a similar painful experience in your past?

CHAPTER 12

The monster acquires language by eavesdropping on Felix while he tutors a young Turkish woman named Safie who comes to live with them. As the monster studies the exiled cottagers, he slowly learns their language and their emotional responses. The intra-psychic equivalent is that our primitive expression of emotions is transformed by our acquisition of language and life experience.

NOTES FOR CHAPTER 12

1. As our monster grows he changes and adapts to our life, education, and emotional experience.

2. Our monster is an archetype, always present and inexorable.

Question: What types of monsters recur in your dreams? How have these dream monsters evolved over the years?

CHAPTER 13

Chapter thirteen opens with Victor's sentence,

"I now hasten to the more moving part of my story."

(Chap 13, par 1)

This is literary balderdash so that Shelley can fill in back-story rather than actually move the novel along. These middle chapters tediously disclose the family histories of the exiled DeLacy's and their Turkish visitors.

Felix deserves a golden apple award as he manages in the course of a few months to teach Safie, and unknowingly the monster, the core of western literature, history, and philosophy. This tutorial miracle explains the monster's university level education and depth of philosophy. But it has some psychological truth because monsters are intellectual equals to us as they transform throughout our lives in response to our experiences and education.

The sweet young Safie plays beautiful music. Shelley likely chose the name, Safie, as a derivative of Sappho, an ancient Greek poet in exile from Lesbos who wrote love poetry. In the Victorian era Sappho was an image of poetic and artistic refinement often associated with a woman's finishing school headmistress.

The monster's education gives him words to describe his self-loathing. He catches a glimpse of his countenance in a pool of water,

> **"I had admired the perfect forms of my cottagers: their grace, beauty, and delicate complexions: but how was I terrified when I viewed myself in a transparent pool! At first I started back, unable to believe that it was indeed I who was reflected in the mirror; and when I became fully convinced that I was in reality the monster that I am, I was filled with the bitterest sensations of despondence and mortification. Alas! I did not yet entirely know the fatal effect of this miserable deformity."**
>
> **(Chap 12, par 13)**

> **"Of my creation and creator I was absolutely ignorant; but I knew that I possessed no money, no friends, no kind of property. I was, besides, endued with a figure hideously deformed and loathsome; I was not even of the same nature as man...Was I then a monster, a blot upon the earth, from which all men fled, and whom all men disowned. I cannot describe to you the agony that these reflections inflicted on me."**
>
> **(Chap 13, par 17, 18)**

This is the heartbreak of monster self-discovery. The monster has the opposite experience of Narcissus seeing himself. Narcissistic persons cannot see their reflections accurately, thus they exhibit annoying ego-inflated personas without the capacity of evaluating their behavior. Victor's monster in contrast sees his reflection clearly, a painful ego-deflating experience. Narcissus fell in love with his reflection which he thought was another person he wished to be, a metaphor for idealizing his persona.

The monster reacts to his painful self-revelation as do most earnest young men: he works harder to dispel the revelation. A sociopath might go on a binge of criminal acts, but the average Joe wishes to please and fit into society so he puts forth a good effort. The monster starts collecting firewood and vegetables for the family.

Helping Felix collect firewood and food represents the interconnectedness of shadow contents. Strange behaviors often make sense when understood as combined shadow traits acting in concert. Although the monster is hidden from the family, he performs helpful activities to express relationship. Metaphorically firewood is stored fuel, but inevitably the firewood burns to ashes.

NOTES FOR CHAPTER 13

1. The monster is ashamed of himself.

Question: Can you name what feels shameful about your core being that gives you a sense of self-loathing?

2. Our monsters try to atone for their acts through compensation Thus much of our compulsions and charity efforts are outlets of shadow libido.

Question: What activities do you feel compelled to perform that have a primary purpose to alleviate guilt?

CHAPTER 14

S afie's father, a wealthy merchant and Muslim, was convicted and jailed for a contrived offense. Parisians were outraged, particularly Felix who worked for their release. Contrary to Victor's passive complicity in Justine's death sentence, Felix is a social activist, a quality of Victor's shadow of feminine justice. Compassionate Felix visited the jailed Arab, subsequently meeting Safie and, as happens in novels, was instantly hit by Cupid's arrow. Felix abetted Safie's father's escape, provoking the French government to exile Felix's family into the woods of western Switzerland.

Safie's father is evil. He exploits Felix's romantic interest in his daughter for his own selfish agenda of greed. He has no intention of allowing Felix to marry his daughter. He intends to sell her into a harem as part of a plan to re-instate himself in Turkish aristocracy. He is the ultimate dark father of the patriarchy, selfish and abusive to his daughter. Safie's father is thus a parallel character to Victor, a dark father who makes his creature for his aggrandizement only to abandon him.

Shelley's use of exiled families and mistreatment of daughters repeats the theme of the feminine disrespect by the patriarchy. Justine was jailed and executed as a result of religious coercion; Safie is a victim of patriarchal abuse from the legal system, family religion, and her father.

> **"Safie related that her mother was a Christian Arab, seized and made a slave by the Turks; recommended by her beauty, she had won the heart of the father of Safie, who married her. The young girl spoke in high and enthusiastic terms of her mother, who, born in freedom, spurned the bondage to which she was now reduced. She instructed her daughter in the tenets of her religion, and taught her to aspire to higher powers of intellect, and an independence of spirit, forbidden to the female followers of Mohammed. This lady died; but her lessons were indelibly impressed on the mind of Safie, who sickened at the prospect of again returning to Asia and being immured within the walls of a harem, allowed only to occupy herself with infantile amusements, ill suited to the temper of her soul, now accustomed to grand ideas and a noble emulation for virtue. The prospect of marrying a Christian, and remaining in a country where women were allowed to take a rank in society, was enchanting to her."**
>
> **(Chap 14, par 8)**

The abuse and oppression of Muslim women has unfortunately changed little in two hundred years since it was written. The split of the feminine in the Muslim psyche allows its cultural denigration of women. The Muslim culture spawns numerous terrorists who are disconnected from their feminine-based function of social justice.

The above passage reveals Shelley's contempt for being a kept housewife, a role imposed upon women of the London gentry. She wrote *Frankenstein* from Zurich during a self-imposed exile. Mary's mother was a vanguard feminist displaying the courage to reject the cultural prescription to be docile. She kept her maiden name and pursued an academic career in an era that granted women little credibility. Mary Shelley achieved independence and literary fame like her mother. Her character, Safie, displays similar courage although her situation is more severe because of her culture and evil father. To live authentically demands immense courage. Although

Frankenstein is primarily a tale of the male shadow, Safie's story illuminates cultural taboos toward women. A woman's shadow "monster" is often a positive source of libido, which if not accessed, becomes a source of depression.

Like Victor's monster, Safie is hiding out and watching, planning her escape and revenge. Felix will assist her, as he represents Victor's latent capacity to rebel against his father's dictums.

> *The dreamer is a doctor. Two patients come in with eye cancers of the retina which are melanomas. One is a middle age woman, the other an old and kind black man. The doctor quickly begins studying laser surgery to preserve their vision.*

The dream's anima figure (unknown woman of the same age as the dreamer) is paired with a positive father-complex (kind elderly black man.) Anima with father-complex is a common pairing. The dreamer is interested in restoring their vision: i.e., giving hope and consciousness to anima and shadow masculine contents. Earlier the pairing of the inner child with the archetype of feminine justice was present in the deaths of William and Justine.

Awareness of archetypal pairings can be useful to access unconscious libido. For example, when addressing a problem involving a father issue, it may be helpful to recruit the feminine feeling function to augment the analysand's resistance to the power of his father-complex. Similarly when a block in anima expression is present, it is often fruitful to search the father-complex for the origin to the block. Safie's father's control of her life is a metaphor for the father-complex blocking anima expression.

Persephone is a classical myth exemplifying depression caused by a controlling patriarchy. She is the daughter of Demeter that is abducted to the underworld by Hades. This is a complex mythological image of the abduction of a woman's power by the masculine, her dependence upon her mother, and the challenge for a woman to live with men and family in a patriarchal world.

Safie's father may actually have love for her, but his cultural beliefs supersede any acceptance of her need for independence:

"He loathed the idea that his daughter should be united with a Christian."

(Chap 14, par 12)

He is cursed by duty as a Muslim father to control his daughters. Reflection and caring for her individuality are blocked. If he were interested in therapy to improve his father-daughter relationship, recruiting his feeling function (love for his daughter) might lead him to accept his daughter's Christian agenda. This would require he find the personal permission and the courage to consciously decide to reject the patriarchal script that refuses independence to women. The non-reflective man will simply quit therapy because his cultural structure is inviolate.

Safie's father restricts her soul by imposing his religion over her Christian preference. Much worse is his evil plan to sell Safie to an Arabian harem. He manipulates Felix with a bogus promise of permission to marry Safie if he helps him escape from the French prison. Felix does so and risks his life transporting Safie's father to Livorno (Leghorn), Italy, which means city of life.

The French government retaliates against the escape by arresting Felix's sister and father. Agatha and her father are tried and convicted although they personally have committed no crime. The patriarchal logic of punishing an innocent woman for a man's crime recapitulates the masculine psychological process of denigrating the feminine. Tribal and Muslim societies to this day may punish a female family member who is raped. The rejection of the feminine function of justice and compassion results in the demonization of women with "justified" vengeance. An observer outside the culture is aghast by the twisted logic. Christianity has a similar legacy in witch burnings.

After four months in jail, Felix, who values relationships, returns to Paris and offers himself in exchange for the release of his father and sister. He is a man with intact feminine-based justice. The state settles the matter by confiscating all of the family's assets and exiling them from France. Aha! The real agenda of the French patricians is revealed: to confiscate the DeLacy's assets as they did to the Arab family.

Xenophobia is the fear of the alien. The ego fears the shadow.

Collectively the shadow of the culture is projected upon other nationalities. Once a foreign group is identified as "the other," it becomes the recipient of abuse. The answer to the question, "Why can't we all get along?" is that until we can accept and live harmoniously with the alien (monster) inside, we will continue to make war with aliens in the outer world.

Once free in Italy, Safie's father regains access to his fortune and arranges to ship his daughter back to Turkey before she and Felix can get married. He puts his sold-to-the-harem daughter into a coach headed for Turkey. He treats her development into a beautiful young woman as appreciation of stock ready to sell for capital gains. While smiling apologetically, he explains that because Felix's family has lost all their assets, he can no longer consent to the marriage of his daughter to a pauper. Some gratitude!

Why do patriarchies fear women, designate them as evil, and persecute them? It is because women carry the feminine energy of men that is dangerous to the power structure of the patriarchy. Justice and sensitivity for fairness and compassion would dissolve a system based on exploitation. Safie's father's justifies selling his daughter into harem as protecting the Muslim culture from Christianity, but good business is his real agenda.

The moral of *Frankenstein* according to traditional literary interpretation is that stealing the divine creativity of life is evil. Victor thus expresses man's evil nature by creating a murdering monster. Shelley looks to the great philosophers for guidance to rehabilitate the evil nature of man. The monster's interest in the texts of Felix's studies expresses this hope:

> "**These wonderful narrations inspired me with strange feelings. Was man, indeed, at once so powerful, so virtuous and magnificent, yet so vicious and base? He appeared at one time a mere scion of the evil principle, and at another as all that can be conceived as of noble and godlike.**"
>
> (Chap 13, par 15)

Reconciling evil and good is a murky endeavor, but the monster is on the right track to accept and engage both consciously. The traditional cultural approach is to reject shadow contents as unredeemable evil. Taboos, culturally defined evil, are established that protect the power structures of church, government, and property owners.

Societies too have shadows that by definition cannot be seen. The demands for cultural cohesion are so strong that when a government is committing evil, its citizens cannot recognize it. The atrocities of Nazi Germany are an example. Women are hidden behind veils and burqas in some Muslim countries because they have been labeled as carrying the evil of lust. Christians persecute homosexuals. The U.S. actively tortures captives, while government leaders proclaim, "The U.S. doesn't torture." Collective reflection is not only difficult; it is disallowed and considered unpatriotic. To suggest that the U.S. is anything but a cowboy in a white hat is an anathema to an American psyche that refuses to recognize its history of supporting despotism in third world countries: e.g. Marcos, the Saudi royal family, Noriega, the Iranian Shah, and others. Americans cannot accept the parts of our consumerist culture that exploit the poor, damage the environment, and promote wars for the largesse of oil producers. President George W. Bush's administration fabricated the terror of "weapons of mass destruction" as justification to attack Iraq. The United States boasts of supporting human rights; however, it has inadequately addressed slavery, the American Indian genocide, and its bombings of civilians during WWII in Germany and Japan. The American persona is unable to admit the truth that most of the perpetrators of 9-11 were from Saudi Arabia where an oil-rich royal family rules in lavish wealth while a majority of Saudis live in subservient poverty. This dictatorial oligarchy has the complicit support of the U.S. with all respect for human rights dutifully ignored. Our collective shadow begs for us to acknowledge and dialogue with it, as does Victor's monster. Without a dialogue our un-exposed shadow will continue to inflict injustice.

En-route to her future sex-slave owners in Turkey, Safie's attendant takes ill and dies. Safie escapes and returns with determination to find Felix. Parallel to Mary Shelley, she is a daughter who spurns her father's dictums in pursuit of true love.

Relating the story of Felix and Safie to Victor moves the monster to tears. The monster feels sorrow not only for the exiled family but self-empathy for his own exile from Victor. Self-empathy is libidinous and may fuel compassion; it also may erupt violently as revenge, as shown in the following example. A wife enters a man's study and asks him to mow the grass. He erupts into anger, slams his book on the desk, and leaves the house. The wife is left with her mouth open, clueless as to what provoked him. The man's monster has downloaded rage from the past, particularly toward his parents who would issue a list of chores he had to perform at times when his inner child wanted to play.

NOTES FOR CHAPTER 14

1. The personal monster is also an agent for the collective monster.

Question: How have you been enlisted to put aside your sensitivities to exploit those below you in order to bolster the power or wealth others in government, church, or industry?

2. The patriarchy is aligned with traditional churches and culture. One must be vigilant in personal beliefs from cultural tenets and reject demands to repress the libidinous needs of the Self.

Question: What rule, restriction, or taboo from your religious training makes you feel empty?

3. The differentiation of evil from good is a complex process. Every action and entity has both good and evil aspects.

Question: What social program do you strongly support? What are the bad effects of that program?

4. There is often a pairing of archetypes in the unconscious. The father-complex commonly blocks the feminine functions of feeling and justice.

Question: Did your father train you to disregard the feelings of others and how does this cause you to mistreat them?

5. The monster is an agent of retribution for repressed archetypal energies.

Question: What is your favorite mode of vengeance?

6. The collective monster is omnipresent.

Question: How do you abet governmental, church, or business policies that exploit others?

ne August afternoon the monster finds a student's leather case that is filled with books: *Paradise Lost*, Plutarch's *Lives*, and *The Sorrows of Werter*. The monster comments on Werter.

> **"The disquisitions on death and suicide were calculated to fill me with wonder."**
>
> **(Chap 15, par 4)**

Freudians name the fascination with death "thanatos," the death instinct. It can manifest as a desire kill self or others. Because death is culturally shunned in western culture, thanatos is generally a shadow concern and naturally is attached to the monster. Suicide is a pact of mutual vengeance between the monster and the ego. The ego experiences despair and loss of libido that originates from the suffering of repressed unconscious parts of the Self. The monster and ego conspire to alleviate the internal suffering and to maintain the ego's control through suicide.

Of *Paradise Lost* the monster comments how his relationship with Victor mirrors that of Adam with God,

> **"The picture of an omnipotent God warring with his**

creatures…struck…similarity…to my own [situation].
Like Adam, I was apparently united by no link to any other
being in existence; but his state was far different from
mine in every other respect. He had come forth from the
hands of God a perfect creature, happy and prosperous,
guarded by the especial care of his Creator; he was allowed
to converse with, and acquire knowledge from, beings of
a superior nature: but I was wretched, helpless, and alone.
Many times I considered Satan as the fitter emblem of my
condition; for often, like him, when I viewed the bliss of
my protectors, the bitter gall of envy rose within me."

(Chap 15, par. 7)

The passage suggests that the monster's vengeance is inevitable
because like Satan, he is judged unredeemable. Pope Benedictine
repeatedly warns against secularism, strictly demanding obedience
to Catholic dogma. There is no mythology for rehabilitating Satan,
only destruction at the end of the world.

There is hope that a new god-image (religious container) will
evolve to include incorporating one's shadow. In religious words
hell and heaven will be united; in psychological terms humans will
be allowed to experience the joy of wholeness. Victor's monster
experienced joy when Felix's blind father accepted him.

"How can I thank you, my best and only benefactor? From
your lips first have I heard the voice of kindness directed
towards me; I shall be forever grateful; and your present
humanity assures me of success with those friends whom
I am on the point of meeting."

(Chap 15, par 33)

Blindness represents shutting down the ego and allowing the
inner introspective work of relating to the monster. Unfortunately
the rest of the family is not blind to the monster's ugliness, and when
Felix, Agatha, and Safie return they run in horror, vacating the cabin
permanently. Embracing your shadow libido will not be encouraged
by the cultural adherents.

Although Shelley's novel suggests that the collective psyche in

190

1818 was incapable of a monster relationship, more hope exists today for such a relationship. Justine, then powerless before the Church, could reject it now. Only a fortuitous death saved Safie from the harem; fortunately, more laws exist today to protect women from sexual slavery. Victor lacked both the ego development for accepting his monster and an available skilled therapist. Two centuries hence, Bueler, Freud, and eventually Jung have discovered depth analysis to offer contemporary man a tool to construct a relationship with the unconscious. The "therapy movement" of today signifies an evolved willingness to tackle the monsters within our psyches.

NOTES FOR CHAPTER 15

1. The monster has an agenda and specific needs.

Question: What do you sense is something you need to incorporate into your life that has always seemed taboo?

2. The unconscious will pull our attention to images and events to help it fulfill its needs.

Question: How are you drawn to situations or activities that give your devil his outlet?

3. Suicidal thoughts arise from a despairing repressed shadow. It may trick the ego into a vengeful pact to kill the body, bringing peace from despair and allowing the ego to maintain control.

Question: When depressed or angry do you fantasize about killing yourself, others, or both (murder-suicide)?

4. A problematic hurdle in shadow work is the Western splitting of good and evil along with the belief that evil contents cannot be rehabilitated.

Question: Image a person you feel is evil. Can you identify parallel traits in yourself? Can you envision framing those traits as acceptable?

5. The evolving transformation of the collective god-image is occurring with the therapy movement that values the individual psyche above the dictates of the church.

Question: In what ways did your religious tradition devalue your individuality?

CHAPTER 16

The monster's elation during his interchange with the blind father is cut short when the family evacuates; so the monster too abandons his pigsty and resumes his search for acceptance. Sadly he receives more scorn and physical abuse. One day the monster approaches a five-year-old boy to befriend him. The little boy calls him a hideous creature and threatens to have his father, "M. Frankenstein," deal with him. Upon hearing that the boy is the brother of his creator, the monster's anguish boils over. The five-year-old continues ranting disparaging remarks until the verbally abused monster attempts to silence him, inadvertently strangling the boy. The strangulation exhilarates the monster:

> "I gazed on my victim, and my heart swelled with exultation and hellish triumph: clapping my hands, I exclaimed, 'I, too, can create desolation. My enemy is not invulnerable; this death will carry despair to him, and a thousand other miseries shall torment and destroy him."
>
> (Chap 16, par 32)

Eureka! The monster has discovered the exhilaration of destructive revenge. Personal suffering can be ameliorated by attacking others, spewing hostility, and delivering rudeness. Transferring pain to another is why abused children become abusive adults. The pain of the priest whose homosexuality has no outlet is soothed with molestation of an altar boy. A responsible method to decompress suffering is to share our misery through conversation. We feel better in the presence of sympathy.

Immediately following William's murder the monster spies the sleeping Justine. He imagines that she will loathe and rebuke him if awakened. This imagined rebuke enrages him and evokes a paranoid logic to strike preemptively. The monster plants the locket containing the painting of Victor's mother into Justine's pocket. He calculates that she will be implicated as the boy's murderer. This second evil act brings him greater delight than the strangling of William.

The monster's paranoid logic resembles confessions of serial killers. The killer fixes his attention on a random woman. Next his imagination projects upon her some evil potential that may be sexual luridness, social deviancy, or an intention to disrespect him. The killer may imagine his victim is plotting injustices against him, such as a mocking rejection to a sexual advance. The "evil bitch" deserves to be tortured and murdered. Murdering her brings the killer the delight of giving her what she deserved. To sustain his joy the ritual killer may photograph her corpse or take a souvenir of her belongings or body parts.

NOTES FOR CHAPTER 16

1. The monster's capacity for revenge is heightened by actual or imagined rejection and persecution.

Question: What rejection or slight from others triggers your desire for revenge?

2. The monster discovers the joy of unleashing his vengeance.

Question: Do you experience joy from revenge?

3. In the monster paranoid logic pre-emptive strikes will protect him from future abuses.

Question: Do you routinely tease your spouse or child or ridicule a co-worker? Can you equate these acts with similar acts when you have been teased or ridiculed?

CHAPTER 17

The monster concludes his narrative with a request that Victor construct a female mate for him, an outlet for his relationship needs. In return he promises to live peacefully in exile.

"My vices are the children of a forced solitude that I abhor; and my virtues will necessarily arise when I live in communion with an equal. I shall feel the affections of a sensitive being, and become linked to the chain of existence and events, from which I am now excluded."

(Chap 17, par 11)

"What I ask of you is reasonable and moderate; I demand a creature of another sex, but as hideous as myself; the gratification is small, but it is all that I can receive, and it shall content me. It is true we shall be monsters, cut off from all the world; but on that account we shall be more attached to one another. Our lives will not be happy, but they will be harmless, and free from the misery I now feel. Oh! My creator, make me happy; let me feel gratitude towards you for one benefit! Let me see that I excite the sympathy of some existing thing; do not deny me my request!"

(Chap 17, par 5)

"My vices are the children of a forced solitude that I abhor" is Shelley's eloquent distillation of the essential monster problem: repressed libido. The female mate is a metaphor for an engagement of a man's ego with the inner landscape of his neglected feelings. The feminine is our watery flow of life. Without its presence a man is dry and isolated. He yearns for meaning. He is a suffering fisher-king who is unable to find the grail of contentment.

The monster senses a softening in Victor's position.

"If you consent, neither you nor any other human being shall ever see us again: I will go to the vast wilds of South America...The picture I present to you is peaceful and human, and you must feel that you could deny it only in the wantonness of power and cruelty. Pitiless as you have been towards me, I now see compassion in your eyes; let me seize the favourable moment and persuade you to promise what I so ardently desire."

(Chap 17, par 6)

Two-thirds of the way through *Frankenstein* Victor reaches this fork in the road: whether or not he can trust establishing a relationship with the monster. The monster offers a win-win situation: Liberate the shadow energy and Victor will receive a libidinous outflow of life-enhancing energy, in return the monster will forego murder and havoc. South America in Shelley's era was considered a primitive jungle, an allusion to the Garden of Eden where man roamed free of judgment. We need enough expression of our primitive human nature to prevent neurosis.

The monster understands that his female partner will be a "hideous" creature like himself. She is a metaphor of a workable relationship between a man and his shadow that is fraught with uncomfortable messiness. The outer world, particular other men, will likely judge the male expression of feelings as hideous.

Why should the relationship with the inner feminine appear "hideous" to men? First, it makes a man feel unmanly. The watery flow of emotional affect overtakes a man and he feels weak, not himself. He feels his ego machismo is diminished, and he is ashamed. Second, a man is terrified by the loss of ego control. When feelings flow, they tend to flood a man. He feels like he is drowning in a forty-foot tidal wave of craziness. He cannot concentrate. His ability to think is washed away, leaving him desperate and grasping for a life raft. Or he reacts like a cat in the bathtub, angry and wishing to escape. He fears he will never recover; instead he will remain a babbling idiot.

A friend witnessed a man's strong emotional flooding. She had been dating a man for three months. The couple predictably had reached a level of bonding for which she wished to clarify the state of their relationship. She asked the man about whether they should date exclusively or remain open to date others. The man immediately began stuttering and accused her of trying to pressure him. He became angry and left. The woman watched him storm off, leaving her open-jawed and confused.

The man was reacting to being flooded by multiple feelings. Was she letting him know she was dating other men: Jealousy? Was she trying to restrict him to an exclusive relationship: Anger at feeling controlled? Was she saying that she would no longer date him unless he intended to marry her: Fear of commitment?

For the woman this was a conversation about openness and clarity in their relationship. For the man, it was an ocean storm: too many huge waves of over-powering emotional energy. Anger and escape are his limited emotional options because he lacks an ability to hold in consciousness his active feelings without decompensating. The man has his child, his monster, and his feminine functions repressed in his unconscious. The monster, being most powerful, erupted to save the terrified inner child from jealous abandonment and the immature feminine from control and commitment. The destructive flight in anger resulted in the woman ending the relationship because "his anger scares me."

A therapist could help this man to separate his feelings of jealousy, fear of commitment, and fear of losing his autonomy. Men generally have had poor training at experiencing multiple emotions while remaining in conversation. Punching the wall is much easier than explaining why you are angry. Because women are more adept at sustaining multiple emotions, they have difficulty understanding this incapacity of men.

Achieving this feminine quality of emotional competency for men is an ancient quest. In the biblical creation story it is God who notices that Adam needs a female companion to assist him. In *Frankenstein* the monster lets Victor know a female companion is necessary. Victor reluctantly agrees to create this companion and the satisfied monster scurries away across the ice fields. Victor weeps at the horror of creating another monster, i.e., acknowledging and expanding the expression of his shadow.

A common archetypal image of isolation is the ice field. Isolation is a cold feeling experienced by a man out of touch with the inner characters of his soul. The *Iceman Cometh*, a play by Eugene O'Neill, captures the meaninglessness in a man's life when too little of the Self's totality is realized. The setting is a bar that attracts lonely defeated men who live in remorse because of lost opportunities. The despairing bar patrons idolize the coolness and bravado of a man nicknamed Iceman. Because their own egos have failed to bring meaning in their lives, they project what little remains of their psychic energies upon Iceman. Iceman comes to the bar one day to confess killing his wife. The metaphor is that the Iceman has killed the feminine side of himself: his soul is dead. He hopes to warn the other men that unless they learn from his example their souls are also in mortal peril. Similarly, Victor's warns Walton against his dangerous course because he will end up like Victor: causing the deaths of those dear to him.

Ice shelves along with cold air, ice, snow, and frozen landscapes are common dream motifs of men struggling with a lost inner feminine relationship. Here are several:

> *The dreamer is standing outside a mansion and he learns that the house and contents must be moved across a lake. Snow is on the ground and also on the lake. He notices a man swimming in the lake so it cannot be frozen solid. The dreamer and unknown others of the house load up the house*

contents into covered wagons, but there is no way to get them over the water.

The house occupants and contents are images of the Self's totality which must get moved across the almost-frozen water, representing the dreamer's coldness toward the unconscious. The house contents may also include the family baggage that the dreamer must sort through and perhaps discard to cross the water. The inner characters and their baggage are transported in covered wagons, i.e., hidden in the unconscious. The wagons are slow-moving, primitive vehicles implying that the move across the lake will be a pioneering journey for the dreamer. They connote the slow process of becoming conscious of the Self. The lone swimmer, a shadow libido image, is in peril, but is continuing to stay afloat in the waters of the unconscious.

This dreamer is walking about the outside of a house in winter. Many people are lounging about the grounds. The sun porch and the first floor windows are open. He thinks he should close the windows.

This man must work on his resistance to opening the windows and experiencing the sun porch, the home of the Self. His ego resistance is twofold: he wants to close the windows; and he is annoyed at the unknown persons lounging about the grounds of his house. Keeping the windows closed is an image of rejecting discovery of his unconscious contents. The unknown persons are characters that comprise the totality of his psyche. They are idle, not being used appropriately. The dreamer describes the time as winter, i.e., his ego feels a cold dreariness. However, the other characters are acting like it is summer.

The dreamer is skiing and ends up at the bottom of a hill. He realizes that the hill is steep and covered with snow. The hill transforms into a very slick ice-covered concrete sheet that he cannot ascend.

Ice, coldness, and loneliness are the images of men in despair. The above dream image of the skier sliding down into an abyss is frightening. This man is like Victor Frankenstein on the glacial shelf. He is at a soul-endangering point of his life. He is stuck in a cold valley. He needs an inner relationship to his feeling function. Optimistically this dreamer had a concurrent dream:

> *The dreamer is outside and notices a very small puppy that fits into his hand. It is very frail, but the dreamer intends to take it home. He hopes it doesn't die because it is so small. The dreamer seeks a baby bottle to feed it. He asks his wife if they have a baby bottle anywhere.*

The endangered tiny puppy is an image of the man's Eros, fragile but with natural animal libido and playfulness. It may be saved by nurturance that will require the wife/anima's assistance. In working with men, the neglected feeling function is fragile. Often it is expressed in dream figures of small girls, animals, or dependent persons. The therapist should point out the fragility of the image and encourage its protection. This dreamer has little contact with his own feeling function that is projected upon and carried by his wife, thus his immediate reaction is to ask his wife for help. This is not pathologic; it merely shows the psychic state of the man's anima relationship. Asking for help is sign of maturity. It is a motif of many fairy tales. Helping feminine characters in a dream connote the ability to reclaim his anima.

At times analysands have great difficulty recalling dreams. Evocative active imaginations or other techniques can help the analysand discover areas of his discontent. Mandala work is another technique that can be used when a man is stuck and unable to recall his dreams.

Mandala is a Hindi word that means magic sacred circle. The analysand is put into a reverent and meditative state for inner reflection. The mandala is then created under the meditation leader's guidance. The man is instructed to draw, in the left side of the circle, an image of what needs to be changed (left behind). In the right side is placed the goal of the future (right direction). At the bottom (unconscious libido) is imaged the resources of the transformation; and at the top (spiritual connection), the collective link with the man's personal process. At the center is placed what feels appropriate. As an example, included below is the first mandala which I drew.

While this process is unlikely to produce items for the National Gallery, it is a valuable tool in psychotherapy. Created in 1992, during a therapeutic transition in my life, I placed my current psychic status on the left. I am sitting naked on an ice block. My therapy is represented by the melting ice-block. In the center is an image of my core Self which is embryonic in the sense that my ego-Self connection was in its earliest stages. I had no idea at the time how to interpret the right-sided image—my Self's goal. Now it is easy to see that I have a feminine figure in what may be considered a garden, like Paradise, a place of peace and natural life. The snake-like animal in the present corresponds to the snake in Eden, and represents my monster as a transformative energy of knowledge. This mandala prescribes a journey to bring into the conscious garden my shadow-monster snake along with my feminine-anima.

The point of presenting this mandala exercise is to make the analysand aware of this exercise in the therapeutic toolbox. Mandala creation can be useful when the analysand is confused or blocking his memories. Mandala technique is a cousin to drawing dream images. The evoked images are powerful because the Self communicates primarily through images. A note of advice: interpretation of mandala images, dreams, or active imaginations may be difficult or unclear for years, so patience is required. Individuation is simply hard work, however it is tackled.

My drawing of a naked man on the ice-block is similar to where we left Victor at the glacial home of the monster. Like Jesus in the Gethsemane garden, Victor begins to weep. Weeping is a detail worth noting for it re-emphasizes the grief and the concomitant potential for suicide that monster work evokes. Victor returns home amid his monster work in despair and confusion about having promised to create a female monster:

> "Thus I returned home and entering the house, presented myself to the family. My haggard and wild appearance awoke intense alarm; but I answered no question, scarcely did I speak. I felt as if I were placed under a ban—as if I had no right to claim their sympathies—as if never more might I enjoy companionship with them. Yet even thus I loved them to adoration; and to save them, I resolved to dedicate myself to my most abhorred task. The prospect of such an occupation made every other circumstance of existence pass before me like a dream, and that thought only had to me the reality of life."

> (Chap 17, par 17)

NOTES FOR CHAPTER 17

1. The despair of disintegration in the male psyche is often a lonely existence and imaged in dreams as living on deserted ice.

Question: Have you dreamed of an icy or frozen location?

2. Ignoring one's shadow is destructive. Engagement will result in a hideous journey, but give birth to a joy of personal totality. It is a requirement for authentic wholeness.

Question: What shadow activity, such as clandestine sex or thievery, have you engaged in but feel ashamed to admit even to yourself?

3. Blocks to relating to the unconscious include:

   A. Feelings of unmanliness

   B. Disorientation and shame

   C. Sensation of losing ego control, "going crazy"

   D. Fear of flooding or being lost in uncontrollable emotions

   E. Humiliation and ridicule from others.

   Exercise: For each item above give an example of your own experience.

4. A useful technique in therapy can be mandala work, one type of guided imagery. It may clearly define the current psychic state, the goal, and the blockage that is stalling the analysand.

Suggestion: Create a mandala, preferably under the guidance of a therapist skilled in mandala work.

   1. Establish a meditative mood and environment.

   2. Ask the unconscious to draw a circle.

      A. In the left quadrant draw your current state.

      B. In the right quadrant draw what needs to occur.

    C. In the top quadrant draw the connection of you to the collective.

    D. In the bottom quadrant draw your personal resources.

    E. In the center draw what feels central at the moment.

    F. Have it interpreted by someone competent in mandala work.

5. Symbols and images of Paradise such as gardens are often prognosticators of achieving progress toward individuation.

Question: Can you recall dreams with garden images?

6. The feminine feeling function is a key element of constructing a personal Paradise and is often represented in dreams of unknown women.

Question: Can you recall an unknown woman in your dreams?

CHAPTER 18

Victor is distracted, obsessing over his promise to create a female monster. His family misinterprets this as depression. A man struggling with transition like Victor may outwardly appear depressed. The Prozac his doctor prescribes is unlikely to help because he is exhausted from the enormous energy of his inner work. He may neglect eating and sleeping while voraciously reading self-help books. It is a lonely task. He needs patience and support; unfortunately, he often receives criticism and ridicule.

Victor is torn between whether to risk the monster's revenge if he fails to make him a mate, or to cause new murders from doubling his monster creations. A man in transition fears the creature he may become if he unleashes his unconscious desires, while knowing he must abandon his old life. During this period in my life I worried about losing income and social status if I left medicine to actively pursue creative writing. To resolve this angst seek a therapist who has experienced the passage and can validate the ambivalence about inner work and offer encouragement to stay the course. The key questions in choosing a therapist are how much therapy has he done; and has he had a journey equivalent to that of the analysand. My opinion is that a therapist under the age of forty-five is incapable of having had enough life experience and processing time to be qualified to do depth analysis.

Victor decides in favor of creating the female monster and plans to move to England to study the female form under the tutelage of a science professor. Although the professor is qualified to help Victor with anatomy, he lacks the experience to protect Victor from his sense of craziness. It is not impossible but rare for a man to accomplish individuation without assistance. A Jungian analyst from Indianapolis sums up the feelings of many men about this period of analytic transition: "I had a lot of help [Jungian depth analysis]. I couldn't have made it alone. I would have been suicidal." I can echo his comments. Having lost my father to suicide, I worried that I had an inherited predisposition for suicide. Luckily I had a seasoned Jungian analyst who went to great lengths to convince me that I was experiencing "normal craziness," and that I was capable of independence from my father's legacy of suicide.

Initiating one's engagement with his monster has immediate salutary effects. Victor's health dramatically improves after his meeting with the monster, although he dreads continuing his monster work:

"My spirits, when unchecked by the memory of my unhappy promise [to create a female monster], **rose proportionately."**

(Chap 18, par 1)

The healing aspects of facing the inner monster are real. A sustaining tenet of depth psychology is that the psyche holds the power and capacity for healing and transformation.

Fearing disapproval, Victor is unable to inform his father of his intent to go to England. At vulnerable moments the father-complex is omnipresent and re-surfaces like Godzilla from the sea to sabotage the healing process by blocking self-permission to pursue individuation. If a man is stuck and unable to grant himself permission to separate from his father, he may benefit from watching the movie, *Panic*. William H. Macy plays a son whose father, Donald Sutherland, trains him to be a hit man. The father's evil agenda is obvious to all but the son, who struggles in therapy to give himself permission to disobey his father's dictum to kill on demand.

The father-complex struggle of Kronus and Uranus is embedded in our most basic and oldest mythology dating back over 8,000 years. Castration of the father is the mythic metaphor for recovering the masculine power and creativity that the genitals symbolize. Victor Frankenstein's submission to his paternal edicts is a de-potentiation of his masculine autonomy. Although he is an adult of twenty-seven years, he must deceive his father about his travel plans to England. He makes the journey, which bodes hope for his progress toward individuation.

Overcoming the father-complex, particularly the collective father-complex is such difficult work that 95% of men (by my personal estimate) fail to do so adequately. The collective father-complex includes a conflation of patriotism and religious obligation. Feuds and wars of the fathers reside in the psyches of their sons. The conflicts are irresolvable until the men of both sides give up their religious dictate to kill for the God-given land of their ancestors.

This is the third time this book has visited the father-complex. This repetition is allowed to emphasize *Frankenstein's* display of the relapsing nature and the persistent power of the father-complex for a man.

Victor's improved mood from his decision to construct a female monster is noticed by his father who takes the opportunity to remind Victor of his betrothal to Elizabeth. This is a red flag that Victor has not consciously chosen his own bride, a tragic portent. Whenever a man enters marriage without enough contact with his anima independent from the woman in his life, she is in danger. Victor knows at an unconscious level that before he marries, he must first address his female monster work (psychologically, his anima work).

> **"I listened to my father in silence, and remained for some time incapable of offering any reply...Alas! To me the idea of an immediate union with Elizabeth was one of horror and dismay...I must perform my engagement** [creating the female monster]**, and let the monster depart with his mate, before I allowed myself to enjoy the delight of a union from which I expected peace."**

> **(Chap 18, par 6)**

209

Victor's intuition is functioning here. The word "engagement" is precise. His inner union of masculine and feminine through his monster work is the correct path. He must create a balanced relationship with his shadow and a relationship to his inner feminine before he can have a peaceful relationship with a woman in his outer life. The Self's push for anima integration often comes as dreams of girls or women that require attention, are growing physically, or are asserting leadership such as becoming a boss at a company. For example:

> *The dreamer must sit and watch a movie about a three-year-old girl. The movie is one reel made of delicate cellophane-like material that will crumble easily. The movie is an old black-and-white newsreel like a Shirley Temple film from the thirties. The girl is an orphan. She begins menstruating and tries to use napkins to control the bleeding. She rapidly develops breasts and grows to adulthood. A boy in the background is silent. A voice warns the dreamer that the movie reel is very fragile and can only be watched once or twice.*

This dream has typical features of a young anima figure maturing rapidly. The uncontrolled menses represents the force of the emerging feminine process. Female processes are bodily based. Like childbirth and menses they are spontaneous and unconscious. The ego must simply "go with the flow." Note in the dream that a boy in the background is silent during her transformation. The anima comes into consciousness in her own way. The ego must not interfere. Time is of the essence. The dreamer gets at most two tries at viewing the fragile movie, i.e., learning about his anima presence.

Victor too must heed the time limits of his unconscious and its monster. Confronting his father's influence proves difficult and Victor procrastinates in its execution. He eventually tells his father a lie that his melancholy will be lifted if he takes a holiday. His fib about lifting his melancholy is actually a psychological truth. Lies to parents have a positive and temporizing purpose. The child fears disappointing the parents, but he has enough personal fortitude to transgress their authority. Lies to parents imply a child is struggling for independence in the presence of an active parental-complex, which is why it is so common for adolescents.

Victor's father enlists Henry Clerval to accompany Victor to England. His father's secret agenda is to use Henry to spy on Victor. Victor knows the monster work is his current life's calling. He admirably demonstrates concern for his family's safety during his absence:

> "One feeling haunted me, which filled me with fear and agitation. During my absence I should leave my friends unconscious of the existence of their enemy and unprotected from his attacks...But he had promised to follow me wherever I might go; and would he not accompany me to England? This imagination was dreadful in itself, but soothing, inasmuch as it supposed the safety of my friends...But through the whole period during which I was the slave of my creature, I allowed myself to be governed by the impulses of the moment; and my present sensations strongly intimated that the fiend would follow me, and exempt my family from the danger of his machinations."
>
> (Chap 18, par 11)

Feeling the horrible awareness of the shadow's potential to harm is a sign of shadow work progress. Continuing the difficult work becomes a moral imperative to protect society against its potential evil. Shelley eloquently describes the compulsive nature of unconscious shadow libido in her words "governed by the impulses of the moment."

Victor departs with the hope of this fantasy:

> "For myself, there was one reward I promised myself from my detested toils—one consolation for my unparalleled sufferings; it was the prospect of that day when, enfranchised from my miserable slavery, I might claim Elizabeth, and forget the past in union with her."
>
> (Chap 18, par 10)

A man harbors the fantasy that a woman can cure his soul

and allow him to ignore the existence of his shadow. The typical unconscious deal a man strikes is to expect his wife or lover partner to carry the split parts of himself. "You complete me," is the trite line offered by Tom Cruise in the movie, *Jerry McGuire*, to a woman character played by Rene Zellweger. "You complete me" is a code phrase for "I want to be with you so I don't have to integrate my feminine unconscious." Often a man will marry a singer or artist to carry his split-off creative arts. A man will marry a soft-spoken woman so that he feels free to be an aggressive businessman. He prefers his wife to decorate the house and buy him clothes. This allows him to avoid the sensate tasks of life. The bargain is short-lived and ends in marital strife.

Elizabeth abets Victor's father's plan by convincing Henry Clerval to accompany Victor to England. The coupling of anima with the father-complex re-surfaces. Henry joins Victor en-route and they travel via the Rhine to the Netherlands before crossing to England. Victor continues to relish the sensate qualities of Henry as do many men who prefer thinking to sensation. They would rather design a garden watering system than enjoy the smell of a rose.

> **"Alas, how great was the contrast between us! He was alive to every new scene; joyful when he saw the beauties of the setting sun, and more happy when he beheld it rise, and recommence a new day. He pointed out to me the shifting colours of the landscape, and the appearances of the sky. 'This is what it is to live,' he cried."**
>
> **(Chap 18, par 14)**

Victor is capable of admiring in Henry what he cannot experience for himself. As a woman Shelley appreciates this capacity more than a typical male author, who might have Victor disparage Henry as rather sappy for being distracted by the landscape. Men are more prone than women to devalue and disparage in others the disconnected shadow parts of themselves. For example, an excellent and famous golfer was asked what he thought of women. He responded that they are "irrational" and he "understands nothing about them." The golfer's string of multiple marriages is a result of his failure to observe and appreciate women, and his inner feminine.

NOTES FOR CHAPTER 18

1. The process of therapy or transformation when activated will consume a man's entire concentration. It requires support, but it will likely elicit criticism and ridicule from others who may feel fearful of change in a person or unsettled when a relationship shifts.

Question: Can you identify times when your wife or friends have discouraged your attempts to expose a different side of yourself?

2. The complexes of the unconscious will be activated and resist change. The father-complex particularly is likely to repress changes. The Kronus challenge of overthrowing the father-complex is a pivotal crossroad in a man's therapy.

Question: What is the most significant expectation of manhood responsibility that emanates from your father and does not represent one of your core desires?

3. Shadow libidos such as the anima and the inferior function may present you with an overwhelming push from the unconscious. This massive push of feeling and sensate elements can be construed as imminent insanity.

Question: Can you identify a desire that shames or embarrasses you and has such an intensity that you fear it will make you foolish or crazy?

CHAPTER 19

The two travelers take lodging in London where Victor arranges a laboratory in secret from Henry. Victor says:

"I saw an insurmountable barrier placed between me and my fellow-men; this barrier was sealed with the blood of William and Justine; and to reflect on the events connected with those names filled my soul with anguish.... I saw in Clerval the image of my former self; he was inquisitive, and anxious to gain experience and instruction."

(Chap 19, pars 2,3)

Victor's despondence is his soul's longing for life. Clandestine activities such as Victor's hidden laboratory are a warning sign of an inauthentic life. Surely his best friend would accept Victor's dilemma, but Victor is ashamed of his monster business and refuses to disclose it. The shame and sadness of Victor contrasts to Henry's vivacious authenticity. Barriers of guilt and remorse hinder change. The intractable nature of depression stems from the inability to accept change.

Men with rigid personalities that restrict their options cripple their ability to access authentic joy. They often attempt to feel joy through sentimentality. They may develop a maudlin attraction to a music piece, a car, or a pet. They may praise a singer as being the most fantastic tenor ever, or proclaim a local garden to be the best in the world. Hitler fawned over his dogs and exalted the symphony and the opera.

Shelley inserts an interesting historical side story of Charles I and the English civil war. The king was forced to transform the monarchy and establish Parliament. She describes the pain and bloodshed of gaining liberty and democracy. Dethroning the monarch and establishing a democracy is an apt description of successful monster work. The ego (a monarch) becomes responsive to the shadow family members who are freed from the repression of ego control (establishing a democracy). The bloodshed is the pain of therapy. Victor says about the English struggle for democracy,

"For a moment my soul was elevated from its debasing and miserable fears, to contemplate the divine ideas of liberty and self-sacrifice…For an instant I dared to shake off my chains, and look around me with a free and lofty spirit; but the iron had eaten into my flesh, and I sank again, trembling and hopeless, into my miserable self."

(Chap 19, par 9)

If Victor could liberate his soul, he too would feel the delight Henry experiences in the world; his depression would improve. Monarchs do not abdicate easily. Victor struggles to maintain his commitment to his female monster project. Each person has a unique sensitivity to his complexes. Henry has the courage to forge ahead, being much less affected by his complexes than is Victor. There is no quick fix for Victor or any man. Like Odysseus a man's midlife transformation and therapy often requires ten years to complete the voyage "home" to the Self.

While Henry is discovering London and delighting in its culture, Victor is secretly collecting body parts. The two men receive an invitation to visit a Scottish acquaintance. As Henry and Victor enter Scotland, Victor becomes progressively irritated by distracting social interchanges with strangers. Victor's irritation is a recurring symptom of his depressive mood disorder. I can identify with Victor for I too am more likely to become irritable than catatonic when depressed. Free-floating-anger and road rage are similar active expressions of a depressive diathesis. Other men simply cannot be still; they must get out to the garage or the hardware store. The symptoms differ, but relief requires discovering who (what archetypal character) is begging for expression and creating the irritability.

Victor senses that his unresolved monster work and his bonding to Henry are inexorably linked in some unknown way,

> **"When these thoughts possessed me** [of the monster], I **would not quit** [archaic for leave] **Henry for a moment, but followed him as his shadow..."**
>
> **(Chap 19, par 13)**

The psychological projection of Victor's sensate function onto Henry has become physical. Paradoxically, the mystical grace of joy in life is experienced through one's inferior, least developed personality function. Robert Johnson's book, *Joy*, is a recommended source for an expansion of this concept.

Because Henry has a highly developed sensate function, I cannot imagine Victor being able to hide from Henry all the body parts he has assembled as they travel. Surely sensate Henry would have said, "Victor, you double you baggage daily and frankly the cargo is a tad malodorous, I do say."

A therapist could advise Victor to unburden his suffering by confessing to Henry his monster problem. Asking for help is a milestone in therapy, signaling a new level of maturity in that the ego consciousness can hold multiple possibilities simultaneously. What blocks Victor is his dominant thinking function and its ego-based hubris. The dominant function of the personality is convinced of its capability and it is determined to "go it alone."

> *The dreamer hears the phone ring twice. It rings so quietly that the dreamer is not sure the phone actually rang. He answers and a female voice says, "Get off the set!" The dreamer tries to figure out what play he may be obstructing.*

This dreamer's ego is in the way of some important play. The voice is the anima, the feminine aspect of his Self, and she is telling his ego to step back from control and trust that the evolving drama will enhance his life. Victor is at such a point in his struggle. He must either allow his shadow its time on stage or risk ruining his life's performance.

Victor and Henry part ways in Scotland: Henry travels northwest to socialize, while Victor sets up a laboratory on an isolated north-eastern island. The desolate island has only three houses and Victor is confident no one will disturb his work. This dramatic point propels the remainder of the novel: Will Victor experience joy without Henry and complete his monster project? Psychologically the question is whether Victor can integrate his anima and reconnect with the joy of his inferior function. It is now up to him as he begins assembling the body parts of the female consort for the monster.

NOTES FOR CHAPTER 19

1. The demands of the Self for integration can be inexorable, over-whelming, and unrelenting.

Question: What haunts you as a "before I die" imperative to accomplish?

2. Barriers to transformation include face-saving and associated feelings of guilt.

Question: What prevents you from confessing to a close friend a problem that troubles your soul for which you see no solution?

3. The key to moving forward to a more joyous state of psychic balance is learning to cooperate with our inferior functions that are inaccessible and because they are unacceptable to the dominant functions of our ego.

Question: What are your inferior functions? If unsure, you can hire a psychologist to administer a Myers-Briggs Inventory to test you and discuss the results.

CHAPTER 20

Arduously Victor begins assembling the monster's mate. He remains apprehensive, fearing the unknown consequences of the feminine monster-to-be. One moonlit night his fear escalates to paranoia that the female monster could be more murderous than the original. He also worries that she may be too ugly to please the monster. What if the end result is two raving evil creatures unleashed upon mankind? Two creatures could become millions if the two monsters procreate! The human race might face annihilation and replacement by a race of monsters!

The moon is the feminine celestial body. Under the moonlight Victor experiences "lunacy," the loss of sanity. Paranoia is a common form of lunacy. Toothpaste tubes are imagined to contain explosives. Gated communities, security guards, window bars, and house alarms exist in excess of actual threats. Meningitis cases are reported on the news despite their rarity and minimal contagiousness. Insurance promotions exploit improbable tragedy. Cholesterol is more feared than lung cancer. Weapons of mass destruction that do not exist have resulted in tens of thousands of Iraqi deaths.

The primal cause of paranoia is the existential angst toward death. Everyone must face the reality that nature has refused us an infinite life. Psychologically, this is the evil mother who devours her children, the dark feminine side of nature that eventually returns us to the pleroma. At the deepest level our inability to conquer death causes a terror of the feminine. Consider the following quotation from Jung:

> *"The mother has from the outset a decidedly symbolical significance for a man, which probably accounts for his strong tendency to idealize her. Idealization is a hidden apotropaism; one idealizes whenever there is a secret fear to be exorcised. What is feared is the unconscious and its magical influence."*
>
> *Archetypes of the Unconscious, CW Vol 9, p 192.*

Witches, bitches, Medusa, the lioness, and the mother bear are images of feminine annihilation within the male psyche. Jung's observation explains why we are compelled to split the feminine: it is an attempt of apotropaism, which means to ward off evil. While he is referring to the ego's fear of the unconscious, a splitting of the feminine also establishes an idealized good mother that protects against the dark feminine aspects of sickness, hunger, and vicious emotions like vengeance.

The primal fear of the dark feminine powers evokes strategies to guard against her. The older male may seek to overpower the feminine by controlling women. Patriarchy is a systemic war against feminine power. Although based on a defense against the dark feminine, the good feminine becomes collateral damage. Patriarchy attempts to compensate for its abuse of women by overvaluing feminine aspects it finds pleasurable, such as beauty and nurturing. Women tend to be confused and frustrated by being overvalued for their beauty and gentleness, while undervalued for their other attributes.

Once split, a man either attacks or runs from the evil side of the split feminine.

> *The dreamer is playing golf, gets sleepy, and then departs the golf course to go to a movie theater. The movies are billed as horror flicks. The first movie takes place in a tomb-like concrete enclosure. The movie protagonist (the dreamer) enters the tomb and sees a monstrous mummy of a woman.*

He examines the woman and then tries to climb out of the tomb to the surface.

Playing golf is the dreamer's ego state of male competition. When he goes to sleep the unconscious comes forth. It shows him a movie of himself, a reflective activity. The woman in the tomb evokes his fear of the feminine powers over life and death that he has entombed in his shadow. He reacts by escaping. His therapist should encourage him to remain present by using active imagination and dialoguing with the mummy.

The dreamer is seated with his wife at a café table within a theater. Also at the table is a woman whom the dreamer identifies as an evil back-stabber from work. His wife is in the middle and on the other side of the table is a third woman whom the dreamer identifies as an honest and helpful, who is an assistant co-worker. Something ignites a rage in the dreamer and he grabs the evil woman's hair and begins smashing her head into the tabletop. The dreamer feels no animosity whatsoever at his wife or the good woman, but he wakes up with heavy chest pains.

This dream shows this man's split feminine as a good and a bad woman with the wife in between. His sub-rosa rage is capable of perpetrating shocking violence. In therapy the dreamer likens his experience of seeing the "evil woman" to being a werewolf viewing a full moon. He accurately describes the werewolf metaphor of lunacy. In werewolf stories a light from the full moon (over-powering feminine) ignites a transformation of a meek man into a vicious killer. Werewolf lunacy is the carnage by a man who cannot contain the power of his angry inner feminine, and transforms from a meek gentleman to a violent abuser, discharging the wrath of his enraged anima.

A less intense flooding with feminine emotional power is anima possession. When a man becomes possessed by his anima he acts irritable, touchy, jealous, vain, or sarcastic. Even in times of minor anima possession a man feels uncomfortable. He cannot make the feelings disappear, and doubly unpleasant is that his masculine thinking function becomes inoperable. The man either freezes up or he snaps out in pettiness, leaving his friends to ask, "What is his problem today?"

The ice queen is an image of a frozen male psyche. In the *Chronicles of Narnia,* the witch freezes men into a rigid state of inoperable emotions. In Greek mythology a man who sees Medusa, the snake-haired mythical female monster, is turned to stone, an apt image of possession by the angry anima that renders his masculine ego inoperable.

A man knows intuitively that he harbors an inner angry feminine that is capable of egregious vengeance. His apotropaism is to project his vengeful feminine elsewhere. Unfortunately this usually means a woman in his life is carrying his projection of the angry feminine. Hillary Clinton carries the "bossy bitch" projection for many men. These men hate her intensely because their own inner feminine has the bitchy power to overwhelm their masculine egos.

The Medusa myth teaches us how to deal with the powerful dark feminine. We must not confront her directly because her power can overwhelm the ego and turn us to stone. Instead we must use the mirror of self-reflection. Perseus overcomes Medusa by looking at her reflectively in the protective shield of Athena, the goddess of feminine wisdom. A man under his anima possession uncomfortably feels turned to stone and cannot function. He spews his discomfort to those around him. He must gain the knowledge of Athena to be present with the emotion and use reflection. With practice a man can learn to name his current emotional state and be present without discharging it onto others.

For example, I have occasionally provided expert witness testimony as a pathologist. The rudeness and arrogance of interrogating attorneys irritates and angers me. The attorneys act this way purposefully to unsettle witnesses. My emotional inclination is to get sarcastic and vicious, but I must use the mirror of reflection and say to myself: "He is provoking you. One of his purposes is to get you to snap and lose credibility in the eyes of the jury. You can remain calm while feeling irritated at the same time." I have learned to do the same process when I am angry at my wife and we are in an argument. The goal of anima work is to develop a controlled container for intense emotions. Young men who observe older men practicing this conscious containment of strong emotions obtain a model for their own anima integration.

> *The dreamer has two mirrors. One is brass and one is made of hardwood framing. Also present is a hand-held electronic device to watch a filmstrip that shows the dreamer murdering a woman he knew years ago.*

The device displays the split-off feminine in his psyche imaged by the woman he murdered. Mirrors and filmstrips are devices for reflection. The two mirrors of the dream are a composite symbol of psychic wholeness. The brass mirror represents the masculine (metal) and the wood one the feminine.

Masculine individuation typically requires three paramount psychotherapeutic challenges: accepting the shadow, overthrowing the father-complex, and integrating the anima. For the latter, a technique is to have a man observe how women talk with one another. If a man listens to women converse he may hear how information and feelings are exchanged. Warn him that the talk will seem lengthy and overdone at first, but this is the female way of processing feelings. The man will need patience to appreciate the different pace and flow of the women's conversations. A corollary instruction is to have a man observe and listen to women talking with children. Women endure the time necessary to hear a child's story because assisting the child to process emotions is the goal, not to convey information.

Anima work entails recognizing emotions and learning to name them. Men get little practice in identifying their emotional states. A man needs to be taught how to identify anger, sadness, disappointment, joy, appreciation, loneliness, etc., and to accept the fluctuating nature of emotions. The act of naming an emotional state and allowing it to run its course enables a man to maintain presence during emotional discharge without being swept into an undertow of moodiness. Once he can name an emotion then he can use Athena's shield of reflection to view his inner Medusa. He can ask himself why he is feeling as he does. What inner sacredness is being violated? What has been said or done? What does he need? What does he wish had been done? How can his current flow of emotional energy guide his movement toward a more pleasant emotional state? A man has achieved a high level of maturity when he can remain present and resist urges to attack or escape.

Perhaps the best outcome of anima work is that men acquire respect for women and treat them as individuals instead of projection carriers. My friend, Robert Moore, Jungian analyst in Chicago, says it best: "A man cannot deal with the angry feminine in the outer world until he has a relationship with the angry feminine in the inner world." If a man in therapy is locked into an insoluble angry conflict with his wife, the cure lies in developing a relationship between the man and his angry inner feminine. A man who has developed a conscious peace with his anima won't react with angry retaliation, when he encounters a truly angry and vicious woman (and there are many). He will be calm or simply walk away.

Homophobia is a special expression of fear of the feminine. Men project their feeling function because it feels unmanly. An effeminate homosexual man evokes contempt for the feminine in a man and provokes a macho retaliatory backlash.

A dreamer realizes a loving gay man is present and is surprised to discover that the gay man is his twin. When the dreamer realizes that he is a family member, he becomes more comfortable with homosexuality.

The social structure of dominant men and subservient women inhibits male integration of the feminine. Fear of feminine power causes patriarchal societies to exclude women from organizational leadership. Religious orders refuse to allow women to become head priests. Muslim countries deny women property rights. The glass ceiling in corporations is exclusion of feminine power. Accepting the feminine side of men requires inviting the feminine into the ruling structure of the psyche.

Dramatic tension of *Frankenstein* peaks as Victor develops lunacy at the prospect of completing the female monster. Will Victor renege on his agreement to construct the female monster and cause tragedy? Victor's fear of a reproducing female monster represents a global problem. Men envy the reproductive powers of women. Abortion rights are vehemently resisted by patriarchal structures of religious systems and conservative political parties. The stated justification is an altruistic fetal protectionism, but this pseudo-concern is actually a façade of their patriarchal agenda to suppress the power of women. "Sanctity of life" pronouncements are disingenuous by those willing to kill humans in war, execute criminals, and deny life-saving health care to the indigent. The unconscious motive is to strip women of their gestational power. Patriarchies have a global collective paranoia at a deep unconscious level that women might breed men out of existence. I personally believe Freud's theory that women possess "penis envy" is a projection of his own envy of the female womb. The fear of death projected onto the aborted fetus is the fear within men that the great mother will eventually kill them. Victor suffers this collective paranoia of female power:

> **"He** [the male monster] **has sworn to quit the neighbourhood of man, and hide himself in deserts; but she** [the female creature he was creating in his laboratory] **had not; and she, who in all probability was to become a thinking and reasoning animal, might refuse to comply with a compact made before her creation."**
>
> **(Chap 20, par 1)**

Victor's paranoia triumphs and he impulsively destroys the nearly completed female monster. Whenever a man acts with rage, he has a vengeful wounded feeling function being acted out by his monster. Victor's angry inner feminine is projected upon the female monster and he violently destroys her. Sound familiar? Like a victim of domestic violence?

The male monster, having followed Victor to north Scotland, observes through a window as Victor decimates his hope for a mate. The monster confronts Victor.

> **"Remember that I have power; you believe yourself miserable, but I can make you so wretched that the light of day will be hateful to you. You are my creator, but I am your master—obey!"**
>
> **(Chap 20, par 9)**

Like Victor, each of us has unconsciously created a shadow that during impulsive explosions becomes our master. A cascade of death is thus initiated with Victor's psychologically fatal decision to battle the monster rather than to befriend him. This is analogous to the man who quits therapy once the going gets rough. He is afraid to trust the process.

Before departing, the monster warns Victor,

"It is well, I go; but remember, I shall be with you on your wedding night."

(Chap 20, par 13)

The psychological truth of this statement is frightening; readers, especially women, should shudder. A man's unconscious shadow/monster is destined to wreak havoc in his marital life.

> *The dreamer has agreed to divorce his wife and marry another woman. The wedding is set for Friday. He changes his mind and goes back to his bedroom to tell his wife he doesn't want a divorce. Then he sees a swarm of bees coming out of the ceiling light. When he inspects the light to see if a hive is present, the bees increase in number and transform into rats that run throughout the house in complete chaos.*

This dreamer is on the cusp of reclaiming his feminine by withdrawing his projections from his wife. Rejecting divorce and reconnecting with his wife will improve his marriage, but the dream portends it will be a little messy. As he gains some consciousness (approaches the ceiling light) his feminine aggression (the bees) is not yet assimilated and is running wild like destructive rats, suggesting more marital strife for this couple. Continued work to withdraw his projections and to identify his inner bees (stinging feminine) will help this man. Bears, bees, ants, cats, and lionesses are animals that often signify the aggressive feminine libido in men's dreams.

The monster departs in anger leaving Victor to clean his workroom. Victor's ego has prevailed over his Self's agenda. Victor senses his refusal to engage a relationship with the shadow feminine has severed his connection with humanity:

"I...walked on the beach of the sea, which I almost regarded as an insuperable barrier between me and my fellow creatures..."

(Chap 20, par 17)

Staying on the beach (out of the waters of reflection) has diminished his humanity. Victor loads the corpse onto a small boat and dumps the remains into the sea. The sea is a metaphor for the unconscious and the little boat is Victor's ego that is at the mercy of its winds and tides. Next Victor falls asleep in exhaustion, another metaphor for relapsing into unconsciousness. Being asleep in a boat to drift at sea is an image of a weak ego at the mercy of the collective unconscious. Attending the second half of life in such a state of unconsciousness is a setup for atrocities in one's inner and outer landscapes. Victor's soul is doomed.

The myth of Prometheus ends with two outcomes of divine vengeance that parallel Victor's fate. First, Pandora opens the box of godly gifts that spill out and cause tragedy for humanity. She is left holding the box that is empty except for hope. The tragedy of *Frankenstein* is that Victor's decisions progressively release the vengeance of the monster. Second, Prometheus is punished by being chained to the rock with Zeus' eagles pecking holes in his liver each night. Being bound to a rock and suffering is an apt metaphor for curtailing the soul's creativity. Men may be in jobs in they hate, marriages that deplete their energy, or belong to churches that deaden their souls. Anyone who is depressed and stuck in a soul-killing situation is like Prometheus. Victor has abandoned his creativity and enlightenment. He will spend the rest of his life being eaten away from the inside, figuratively pecking holes in his own liver.

"I banished from my mind every thought (of creating a female monster) that could lead to a different conclusion."

(Chap 20, par 21).

The inability to imagine life changes, the inability to grant oneself the freedom to attempt seemingly unachievable expectations, and the inability to trust the unknown are the seeds of suicidal ideation. A person becomes "disheartened" from failure to achieve his life's goals (true desires of the "heart"). He becomes hopeless when he cannot envision life alternatives. Depressed persons feel the prison walls of misery close in upon them. Victor's next stop is jail.

NOTES FOR CHAPTER 20

1. The emotional parts of a man are feminine in nature.

Question: Can you identify a sense of lifelessness when you withhold emotional expression?

2. There is a great tendency to split the feminine side of a man into good and evil.

Question: Can you identify two women you hate and explain why? Can you do the same for two women you idealize?

3. A man fears being overcome by emotions because it is painful to experience losing ego control. Further a man fears he may commit vicious acts if he unleashes his angry inner feminine.

Question: How do you act when you lose ego control during an emotional outburst?

4. Splitting your feminine results in over-idealizing of some women as beautiful, nurturing, soft, or kind, and demonizing other women as deceptive, cruel, devouring, and murderous.

Question: For the women identified in question #2 can you see an evil side to the idealized women and a good side to those demonized?

5. When men reject relationships with their inner feminine natures, they tend to oppress and abuse women.

Question: Can you identify ways in which you have belittled women?

6. The process of anima integration requires identifying, naming, and tolerating emotional states while employing a masculine boundary to prevent flooding. Maturity is maintaining a conscious presence.

Question: Can you identify times when you have remained present and calm during an uncomfortable and emotionally-charged argument with your wife/girlfriend?

CHAPTER 21

While Victor sleeps off his exhaustion, the winds shift and carry his boat from the Scottish coast to Ireland, where it drifts into a village harbor. He arrives tired and ill, but relieved to touch land. To his surprise and dismay, he is greeted rudely by the townspeople, who immediately remand him to the local magistrate.

The previous morning a strangled man was found on the shore near the village. When the magistrate shows Victor the body of Henry Clerval, he is overwhelmed with grief and takes ill with fever and delirium. Realizing his complicity in the monster's murders, he mumbles that he has killed Henry and the others. The townspeople accept his delirious confession and imprison him.

These events portray two psychological metaphors. First, Henry, the symbolic representation of Victor's inferior function, is dead now that Victor has refused to do his shadow work. Like Lady Macbeth who can "sleep no more," Victor can experience joy no more.

Second, Victor has been thrown into prison, a metaphor for his despair. Shelley describes his depression:

> "The cup of life was poisoned forever; and although the sun shone upon me, as upon the happy and gay of heart, I saw around me nothing but a dense and frightful

darkness, penetrated by no light but the glimmer of two eyes that glared upon me. Sometimes they were the expressive eyes of Henry languishing in death, the dark orbs nearly covered by the lids, and the long black lashes that fringed them; sometimes it was the watery, clouded eyes of the monster as I first saw them in my chamber at Ingolstadt."

(Chap21, par 39)

Individuals often experience physical symptoms to emotional stress in a personally predictive pattern. For Victor the physical component is fevers and delirium. For other men it may mean ulcers, diarrhea (functional bowel disease), or chest pains. Heart attacks are common to hyper-vigilant men who do not reflect and accept change. Men who become workaholics to avoid inner work often die on the job or within a short period after retirement.

In prison Victor weeps regularly, as depressed people do. He is grieving for his family and friends, and unconsciously, for the un-lived parts of his Self. Victor starts ingesting large doses of laudanum, an opiate that is addictive. The drug temporarily eases his pain and helps him sleep. Victor's unconscious retaliates, sending him a barrage of nightmares to get his attention, attempting to reconnect him with his monster.

"My dreams presented a thousand objects that scared me. Towards morning I was possessed by a kind of nightmare; I felt the fiend's grasp in my neck, and could not free myself from it; groans and cries rung in my ears."

(Chap 21, par 43)

Victor has hit rock-bottom and uses increasing doses of narcotics to suppress the assaults from his unconscious. Addictions, particularly of drugs and alcohol, serve two purposes. First, they numb the uncomfortable feelings arising from within, and second, they create a pleasant flow of libido that acts as a surrogate discharge of the imprisoned psyche. "Life-of-the-party" men who become friendly and talkative when drinking are discharging pent up libido. Abusive drunks are not so pleasant, releasing libido in the form of anger and violence. Drugs and alcohol may numb unconscious feelings, but they also numb and inhibit ego control. Drunken behavior is a gold mine for discovery of the suppressed Self.

Victor gradually recovers his physical health but remains despondent. His father is summoned to the murder trial. The receipt for Victor's lodging in Scotland is presented as proof that Victor was out of the country the evening that Henry Clerval was murdered. Victor is released and agrees to accompany his father back to Geneva.

NOTES FOR CHAPTER 21

1. A man's inferior function is a conduit for expressing his joy because it balances his dominant functions.

Question: What activities allow you expression of your inferior function?

2. Physical stress associated with prolonged ego suppression of the unconscious may surface as an illness.

Question: What physical symptoms do you commonly suffer during periods of stress or emotional pain?

3. Addictions and compulsions are poor and dangerous substitutes for direct integration of the unconscious. Addictive behaviors have an origin from unconscious sources.

Question: What are your habitual remedies for self-soothing and what is the root need that is not being met?

CHAPTER 22

En-route home, Victor's father attempts to console him but cannot. Anyone who has dealt with a person in depressive crisis knows there is no simple formula for "cheering him up." Victor experiences self-loathing and is drawn to the worst of his fellow man. Misery loves company if you will.

> **"I abhorred the face of man. Oh, not abhorred! They were my brethren, my fellow beings, and I felt attracted even to the most repulsive among them as to creatures of an angelic nature and celestial mechanism."**
>
> **(Chap 22, par 1)**

Depression acts like a giant set of power brakes stopping the flow of energy to the ego. Anti-depressive drugs can assist mood elevation and libido, but only inner work is likely to achieve a long-term transformation. Victor reflects enough to know he bears responsibility for the deaths of Justine, William, and Henry, yet he cannot bring himself to confess his monster problem to his father or Elizabeth. Victor's ego remains resolved to save face, albeit somewhat contrite.

"I checked, therefore, my impatient thirst for sympathy, and was silent when I would have given the world to have confided the fatal secret."

(Chap 22, par 4)

"Alas, my father, how little do you know me. Human beings, their feelings and passions, would indeed be degraded if such a wretch as I felt pride. Justine, poor unhappy Justine, was as innocent as I, and she suffered the same charge; she died for it; and I am the cause of this—I murdered her. William, Justine, and Henry—they all died by my hands."

(Chap 22, par 3)

His father interprets these self-incriminations as grief-induced hallucinations. Victor's struggle to integrate his monster predictably gets no help from his father. Victor's father is incorrect. Victor is not psychotic. He is like Hamlet, whose "madness" is isolation, self-absorption, and riddled speech: symptoms of internal conflict, not madness. Just as family duty kills the soul of Hamlet long before Laertes's sword penetrates his chest, Victor has committed his soul to its death and it is retaliating.

Hope persists until death, and Victor could still finish his monster work and re-commit to establishing a female partner for the monster. However, the chances for success wane as time passes. The Greek word, kairos, means special time. Kairos for mid-life turmoil has a window of opportunity.

Victor refuses to reconsider his monster work; hence the waters of misery commence their final cataract. He receives a letter from Elizabeth. She uses the most pleasing and polite Victorian prose to grouse about their much-too-long engagement, reminding Victor that she is twenty-six. She questions whether Victor is in love with someone else. She implores him to be a man and confess if he has no passion for her. She delivers the ultimatum: either break the engagement or set a wedding date. She requests that he not answer immediately but that he gives it a proper, serious, and irrevocable deliberation.

Woman eventually get angry and stop carrying a man's anima. Predictably Elizabeth's ultimatum makes Victor more despondent, partly for her calling him to the carpet but also because his Self was never fully invested in their arranged marriage. He is haunted by the monster's threat to accompany them on their wedding night. He concludes that inevitably he, the monster, or both must die.

Victor's ego decides to salvage some dignity by giving Elizabeth her deserved too-long-awaited wedding. Considering her happiness is honorable; however, he knows this will provoke a showdown with the monster. Victor arranges a wedding date with Elizabeth but fails to confide his predicament in her. She displays her feminine intuition as she intuits danger:

> **"But it is your happiness I desire as well as my own when I declare to you that our marriage would render me eternally miserable unless it were the dictate of your own free choice."**
>
> **(Chap 22, par 12)**

Women often know a truth that men cannot feel or admit. Elizabeth knows she is not Victor's free choice, rather a result of his mother's choosing. Marriage is just one of life's issues upon which Victor has failed to reflect. But the profundity of Elizabeth's statement is the psychological truth that our spouses will be eternally miserable unless we choose them freely.

A man will choose a spouse unconsciously to carry his anima projection and mother-complex. This is the fate of the young as they go about the courtship rituals of unconscious bonding. Half of marriages end in divorce as this paradigm fails. Those that survive do so for predominantly two reasons: a religious, family, economic, or social rejection of divorce; or a maturation of couples who take back their projections.

A man's task of maturity is to separate the real woman who is his spouse from his projected anima image in her. Carrying a man's feminine projection will make a woman crazy if she doesn't understand the process. She will become miserable if the man refuses to reach psychological maturity and withdraw his projections. Ultimately she will refuse to carry his anima adequately and strife will ensue.

Withdrawing projections of the anima and parental complexes is the basis for the Imago Therapy of Harville Hendrix. His staff specializes in the pain and anguish of couples caught in these unconscious projections. The exercises in their books and workshops lead couples to write down and discuss how each is like the other's parents, god images, and ideal people. A tenet of the Imago Therapy is that the wife is carrying the man's anima projection and the husband is carrying the wife's animus; and the arrangement will inevitably fail and poison the marriage. The archetypal and inhuman task to carry the soul of another is impossible. The more immature and unconsciousness the projecting spouse is, the more intense will be his or her rage at the other spouse's inadequacy. This rage is the seething vitriol that spews during a nasty divorce.

Victor and Elizabeth forge ahead with wedding plans. They both feel uneasy and have no genuine joy for their upcoming marriage. Their union has become an end-stage ritual devoid of passion, more like the marriage state at mid-life rather than the wedding night. Noticing Victor's moodiness, Elizabeth attempts to comfort him. Victor describes himself as,

> **"...furious and burnt with rage... I neither spoke nor looked at anyone, but sat motionless, bewildered by the multitude of miseries that overcame me...Elizabeth alone had the power to draw me from these fits; her gentle voice would soothe me when transported by passion, and inspire me with human feelings when sunk in torpor. She wept with me, and for me. When reason returned, she would remonstrate, and endeavour to inspire me with resignation."**

> (Chap 22, pars 18, 19)

A man is comforted when a woman expresses his feelings. Like his mother, his wife has the capacity to placate him. But relying on one's wife to the exclusion of one's intrinsic feeling function eventually fails. In modern societies this is commonly played out by men who sequentially marry and then divorce the next wife as soon as her ability to carry his projections fails. *Frankenstein's* warning is that whether from fear or laziness, a man who fails to consciously carry his own anima will bring misery to his wife. For example: a recent newspaper reported that a man purposely crashed his airplane into his wife's mother's house to kill her, himself, and their eight-year-old daughter. In his suicide note he justified his vengeance: his wife's inattention had ruined his life.

Victor's vengeance is focused on his monster. He has become a grumpy old man, filled with free-floating anger. He welcomes death. The wedding, a joyless event, takes place ten days after Victor's returns to Geneva. His father is pleased, i.e., Victor's parental-complexes have prevailed. In contrast, female intuition engulfs Elizabeth with a despondency of foreboding evil.

Victor and Elizabeth plan to honeymoon at the Villa Lavenza, whose name means the wash house. Psychologically they hope the marriage will cure their inner maladies and wash away the past. This is wishful thinking, akin to sparring couples that think having a baby or building a new house will improve their relationship. The couple spends their wedding night at a hotel in Evian, a well-known natural spring and a popular brand of bottled water. The water spring is a metaphor for the forces of the unconscious that are about to gush.

NOTES FOR CHAPTER 22

1. The usual and common structure of relationships is for one partner to carry the unconscious soul/anima/animus of the other partner.

Questions: Are you aware of your wife's failures to carry you anima? Are you jealous when she is not available or has her own success? Does she criticize you for not talking about your emotions? Do you rely on her to make social engagements and shopping decisions? Do you evaluate your own opinions and feelings independently from your wife?

2. Continuing to project one's soul will eventually result in an intense anger toward the partner when she fails to meet those needs.

Question: What actions or inactions by your wife disappoint and anger you? In what ways does she fail or refuse to please you?

CHAPTER 23

In anticipation of his monster confrontation, Victor patrols the hotel grounds armed with pistol and dagger. His firearm is no match for the monster; psychologically his ego is no match for his archetypal monster. He refuses to heed the monster's admonition that he is the ultimate master over Victor.

Victor hears a dreadful scream from his hotel suite. He discovers the limp body of his strangled wife. He sees the monster running away and fires a shot that misses. The gunshot alerts the townspeople who find Victor sobbing over his wife's corpse.

In *Frankenstein* each victim (Justine, William, Henry, and Elizabeth) is strangled or hanged. The metaphor is de-inspiration: they have lost the physical inability to inspire air; Victor's psychological de-inspiration is the loss of spirit.

None of the numerous Frankenstein movies to date has exactly represented Shelley's text as a psychological study of the inner monster. This is not meant to malign the movie industry whose purpose is commercial entertainment. Literature is an introspective medium whereas film is a visual medium. Filmmakers have emphasized the visual horror of the manufactured monster, and down-played the intra-psychic metaphor of the book. Francis Ford Copula's 1991 film is the best attempt at capturing the tragedy of Victor's monster rejection. The wedding night scene in this film is altered from the book in that the monster murders Elizabeth by tearing her heart out of her chest. The tearing out of Elizabeth's heart is a valid metaphor for the heartbreak a woman suffers at the hands of her husband's unconscious monster. A man's monster side will eventually betray a woman and break her heart. As she comes to carry more of his negative anima (witch) than his positive anima (maiden), he is inclined toward infidelity, divorce, or violence. The man fails to see her as a separate unique person and to cherish her, which tears at her heart.

High alert should be signaled when a woman coldly states she hates or no longer loves a man. Not only does it portend that the marriage is unlikely to survive, but most worrisome is that the wife could be in serious danger if her husband is prone to violence. Likely the woman has already conveyed her loathing in her gaze and words. This can cause an unstable man to decompensate in violence or suicidal depression. If he has poor control over his violent nature, he may have the capacity to commit one of the murder-suicides that make the news. When the wife announces she does not love him and is divorcing him, it feels like the end of his world because she is leaving with his projected soul. Commonly he tries for several weeks to "get her back" but soon realizes that she is serious and the marriage is over. Feeling dead himself, he projects that the family is also dead. The wife can be murdered because she deserves punishment. Victor's monster has a similar quid-pro-quo logic: your anima carrier (Elizabeth) dies because you killed mine (female creature), when he strangles Elizabeth.

Worse the man then may project his misery and suffering from childhood onto his children and kill them to protect them from the pain of family dissolution. They are murdered because the father cannot separate his emotional state from that of his children. Sometimes the children are killed out of rage at the mother, but more often the children are conflated with the man's global feeling of death. News reports of domestic homicides typically describe the perpetrator as a helpful neighbor who seemed like a nice man, but he was quiet and kept to himself, i.e., he had expressive difficulty. The police had been called to the house before for domestic battery, i.e., his monster was capable of violence.

Losing the woman who carried his mother-complex causes Victor to lose his animation and feeling connections. Victor returns to Geneva with the horrible details of Elizabeth's death which causes his father to die from grief. Victor loses his energy to interact with the outer world, a metaphor corresponding to his father's death, as the father-complex carries a son's initiative to succeed. The deaths in his family are a metaphor for Victor's total split from his psyche. He is left with his ego as the sole survivor of the internal House of Victor Frankenstein.

Too little and too late, Victor finally confesses his monster creation and the subsequent murders to a police magistrate. This is the valueless death bed confession of a sinner, an ego-serving attempt to unload guilt past the time for atonement. Victor hopes to enlist the authorities to capture the monster. Gone is his opportunity to personally perform the work of relating to his monster. This logic is similar to that of Dennis Rader who sent police clues to direct the arrest of his BTK monster.

Too many men begin dealing with their monsters after too much damage has occurred. A man in mid-life crises may wait until after he has abandoned his wife for a younger woman and the family has been devastated. A grumpy old man goes to his grave scowling at his children because his inner child has died. Men sit stone-faced on park benches without friends or family. Howard Hughes, the aircraft industry mogul, spent his final years as an emotionless recluse, naked and paranoid. Victor's confession does grant him a flicker of relief as he experiences a moment of authenticity.

"This address [confession] caused a considerable change in the physiognomy of my own auditor."

(Chap 23, par 24)

For the soul-dead, the end of life is either meaningless or becomes devoted to evil purpose. Victor chooses the latter, intending to devote his last days to revenge. The police magistrate politely refuses to assist Victor, judging his story as ludicrous. Victor announces:

"You refuse my just demand: I have but one resource;

and I devote myself, either in my life or death, to his destruction."

(Chap 23, par 27)

In departing to chase his monster to its death, Victor berates the magistrate with a flourish of his own Promethean-ego projection,

"Man, how ignorant art thou in thy pride of wisdom! Cease; you know not what it is you say."

(Chap 23, par 29)

Victor plots to stalk and kill the monster, unaware that this is an archetypally impossible task.

NOTES FOR CHAPTER 23

1. Becoming conscious of the anima is the most difficult and usually the last of the major achievements in a man's transformation. Clues that intensive anima work is necessary include: moodiness, irritability, anger, jealousy, and the denigration or idealization of women. Sexual fantasies and dreams of young women, female castration, Amazons, spiders, bears, and acts of seduction are often an invitation to anima integration.

Question: From the list above, which feminine images occur in your dreams?

2. The therapy of anima consciousness includes dialogue with the inner characters who are moody or angry.

Questions: Have you dialogued with angry or moody dream figures?

3. A man's relationship with his woman partner will generally

uncover and reflect the unresolved angry feminine character inside his unconscious.

Question: What buttons can your wife push that immediately anger you?

4. Consciousness requires a man to understand how he projects his emotions onto women to whom he is attracted.

Questions: What type of woman immediately attracts you? Which traits of hers do you have difficulty expressing yourself?

5. An important goal of anima work is the ability to feel and experience anger without committing to acts of rage.

Question: What must you tell yourself in order to remain present while you are angry?

6. A man must accept his female partner as an autonomous person. This means that he exists independent of her. She could leave him tomorrow, or he could leave her, and the world would not end.

Question: Can you honestly say that if your wife left you tomorrow, your life could become ordered and you would not decompensate and feel crazy?

7. The anima, a man's soul, will carry his sense of being alive.

Question: Can you feel that your aliveness emanates from an inner source?

CHAPTER 24

As Victor leaves Geneva "forever" in order to chase down and kill his monster, he visits the graves of William, Elizabeth, and his father. The archetypes of the psyche are immortal, but they feel dead to Victor. He leaves home with money and:

> **"A few jewels which had belonged to my mother."**
>
> (Chap 24, par 2)

Taking her jewels represents the persistence of his mother-complex. Victor's tragedy thus begins and ends with his mother-complex. His mother's death drove him to create the monster; the gold locket with his mother's picture was linked to the first murder, and her jewels remained with him at the end of his life.

The monster's actions have cycled from requesting expression, to resisting the ego's attempt at repression, to enacting revenge. The monster appears at Elizabeth's gravesite. He laughs at Victor, moves close to him, and whispers in his ear,

> **"I am satisfied: miserable wretch! You have determined to live, and I am satisfied."**
>
> (Chap 24, par 7)

The monster has satisfied his libido expression through murder. Victor resolves himself to retribution against his monster. Victor chases the monster down the Rhone, across the Mediterranean Sea, north through the Black Sea and Russia and into the Arctic Islands.

> **"My life, as it passed thus, was indeed hateful to me, and it was during sleep alone that I could taste joy. O blessed sleep! Often, when most miserable, I sank to repose, and dreams lulled me even to rapture. The spirits that guarded me had provided these moments, or rather hours, of happiness, that I might retain strength to fulfill my pilgrimage."**
>
> **(Chap 24, par 12)**

Victor clearly has failed to individuate. Even so, Victor's psyche still attempts healing, offering him images of solace and joy that his ego cannot imagine. The unconscious never gives up. Thus the monster keeps near enough to persist in engaging Victor.

> **"Sometimes, indeed, he left marks in writing on the barks of trees, or cut in stone, that guided me and instigated my fury. 'My reign is not yet over' (these words were legible in one of the inscriptions); 'you live, and my power is complete. Follow me, I seek the everlasting ices of the north, where you will feel the misery of cold and frost to which I am impassive.'"**
>
> **(Chap 24, par 13)**

The path to psychic wholeness is non-linear with ups and downs, twists, and detours. Our shadows wish to become known and be expressed. If they are refused like Victor's monster, they will lead us to those Arctic islands of "ice-o-lation" previously described. Victor's life is end-stage with dwindling rations and a dying team of dogs, representing his instinctual and physical life.

> **"Never will I give up my search, until he or I perish; and then with what ecstasy shall I join my Elizabeth and my**

**departed friends, who even now prepare for me the reward
of my tedious toil and horrible pilgrimage!"**

(Chap 24, par 14)

Joy in the afterlife is a solace promised by most religions to forego
an earthly pursuit of personal authenticity. Modern psychologies,
particularly Jung's depth psychology consider ignoring/ignorance of
the Self a psychopathology that creates suffering. The paradox holds
true for Victor: although he is living according to the edicts of his
parents and a patriarchal society, he is experiencing hell due to an
ignored Self.

Walton provides Victor with blankets and a warm fire aboard the
ship to revive him from the cold. Victor has one final opportunity for
a spiritual resolution. He can tell his story to Walton to persuade him
to turn back from ice floes. Victor addresses Walton,

**"Are you mad my friend? Or wither does your senseless
curiosity lead you? Would you also create for yourself and
the world a demoniacal enemy? Peace, peace! Learn my
miseries, and do not seek to increase your own."**

(Chap 24, par 28)

In a letter to his sister, Walton describes Victor's volatile temper
when Victor blames the monster for his problems. Walton is appalled
and frightened by Victor's vengeance and obsession about killing the
monster. Inappropriate anger is a sign that a man is out of touch with
an unconscious source of libido.

**"Sometimes he [Victor] commanded his countenance
and tones, and related the most horrible incidents with a
tranquil voice, suppressing every mark of agitation; then,
like a volcano bursting forth, his face would suddenly
change to an expression of the widest rage, as he shrieked
out imprecations on his persecutor."**

(Chap 24, par 26)

Walton observes Victor hallucinating, but Walton lacks an

understanding of the psychic reality that the voices he hears belong to "real" beings in Victor's inner world.

> "He believes that, when in dreams he holds converse with his friends and derives from that communion consolation for his miseries or excitements to his vengeance, they are not the creations of his fancy, but the beings themselves who visit him from the regions of a remote world."
>
> (Chap 24, par 30)

Victor laments his destiny:

> "They are dead; and but one feeling in such a solitude can persuade me to preserve my life. If I were engaged in any high undertaking or design, fraught with extensive utility to my fellow-creatures, then I could live to fulfill it."
>
> (Chap 24, par 34)

In response to his sister's letter of concern for his safety, Robert Walton confides to her his dilemma whether to release his crew or to continue the voyage.

> "I write to you encompassed by peril and ignorant whether I am ever doomed to see again dear England, and the dearer friends that inhabit it. I am surrounded by mountains of ice which admit of no escape and threaten every moment to crush my vessel. The brave fellows whom I have persuaded to be my companions look towards me for aid; but I have none to bestow. There is something terribly appalling in our situation, yet my courage and hopes do not desert me. Yet it is terrible to reflect that the lives of all these men are endangered through me. If we are lost, my mad schemes are the cause."
>
> (Chap 24, par 35)

> "This speech (pleas from the crew to turn back) troubled me."
>
> (Chap 24, par 41)

Walton has reached his pivotal moment whether he will reject the crew's pleas to abandon the mission. Several have already perished. Walton feels a push to acknowledge the crew's supplication at the *reflecting* level of his inner psyche. He is vaguely aware of his own peril.

The ego is not pathologic. It is a necessity to guard against psychosis. Those who lack an adequate ego are susceptible to flooding by the unconscious and are at the whims of an uncontrollable sea of emotions. People with inadequate egos, such as those with borderline personality disorder, are unable to separate their reality from others around them. Many individuals cannot hold jobs or maintain relationships because their fragile emotional control perpetually dissolves into craziness. Although ego control is appropriate for the first half of life, it must become a reverent servant to the Self later. The ego becomes pathological when it attempts to create and maintain its own agenda after mid-life.

While Walton contemplates his dilemma, Victor deteriorates, becoming bedridden and hallucinating. In his final act, Victor re-asserts the supremacy of his self-aggrandizing ego and abandons all reflection and change, advising Walton to do the same. In a psychotic rant Victor goads Robert to continue his quest for glory, as it is the *raison d'etat* for his expedition.

> **"You were hereafter to be hailed as the benefactors of your species; your names adored as belonging to brave men who encountered death for honour and the benefit of mankind...Do not return to your families with the stigma of disgrace** [mission aborted] **marked on your brows. Return as heroes who have fought and conquered, and who know not what it is to turn their backs on the foe."**
>
> **(Chap 24, par 41)**

Walton's ego hears exactly what it wants to hear. He recommits to the Arctic mission for glory, ignoring its risks. He dismisses the grief his death would bring to his sister. But when enough ice breaks to free the ship, Walton's heart melts enough to put the crew's welfare above his ambition. Breaking the ice is a metaphor for the cracking of

Robert Walton rigid ego. While Victor is sleeping, (unconsciousness) Walton decides (consciousness) to turn back to England.

The crew is ecstatic and makes a celebratory din that awakens Victor, who chides Walton's decision to turn back. Walton's ego feels this decision is an act of cowardice and shame, but his heart has led him. Following the heart is never easy for a man, and rarely is he encouraged to do so!

Victor declines Walton's invitation to return to England, re-supporting his ego's agenda. He opts to leave the ship, despite knowing that chasing the monster will be fatal.

> **"Alas! The strength I relied on is gone; I feel that I shall soon die, and he, my enemy and the persecutor, may still be in being."**
>
> **(Chap 24, par 51)**

Victor speaks an archetypal truth: forces in the psyche are immortal. The shadow/monster cannot be killed during life and lives on after death in our deeds and relationships. Victor does not survive to further chase his monster, but dies in his cabin. On his deathbed Victor has a glint of insight. He finally acknowledges,

> **"In a fit of enthusiastic madness I created a rational creature, and was bound towards him, to assure, as far as was in my power, his happiness and well-being. This was my duty; but there was another still paramount to that. My duties towards the beings of my own species had greater claims to my attention, because they included a greater proportion of happiness or misery…Farewell, Walton! Seek happiness in tranquility, and avoid ambition, even if it be only the apparently innocent one of distinguishing yourself in science and discoveries. Yet why do I say this? I have myself been blasted in these hopes, yet another may succeed."**
>
> **(Chap 24, pars 51,53)**

Victor is partially correct. He does have a collective responsibility, but he fails to realize that his inability to relate to his personal monster has caused his family tragedies. Carl Jung said that one must find a personal solution to a collective problem. In other words, one must do his individual therapy work because a healthy psyche serves the greater good. Men can do no greater service to the collective than by adequately transforming their personal monster potentials.

Soon after this speech Victor dies in his sleep, a metaphor for his eternal unconsciousness. Walton is awakened by loud roars of pain, and finds the monster grieving over Victor's corpse. Walton rushes to Victor's cabin. The monster is holding the corpse and addresses Walton:

> **"That is also my victim! In his murder my crimes are consummated; the miserable series of my being is wound to its close. Oh, Frankenstein! Generous and self-devoted being! What does it avail that I now ask thee to pardon me? I, who irretrievably destroyed thee by destroying all thou lovedst. Alas! He is cold, he cannot answer me."**
>
> **(Chap 24, par 60)**

The death of Victor Frankenstein is a metaphoric suicide. This is the gut-wrenching tragedy awaiting men who ignore their monsters. They are "cold" and die alone from their own failure of inner work, the reason for *Re-Membering Frankenstein*.

The monster continues to talk to Victor's corpse,

> **"And do you dream? Do you think that I was then dead to agony and remorse?"**
>
> **(Chap 24, par 62)**

> **"After the murder of Clerval, I returned to Switzerland, heartbroken and overcome. I pitied Frankenstein; my pity amounted to horror: I abhorred myself. But when I discovered that he, the author at once of my existence and of its unspeakable torments, dared to hope for happiness; that while he accumulated wretchedness and despair upon me, he sought his own enjoyment in feelings and passions from the indulgence of which I was for ever barred, then impotent envy and bitter indignation filled me with an**

insatiable thirst for vengeance. I recollected my threat, and resolved that it should be accomplished. I knew that I was preparing for myself a deadly torture; but I was the slave, not the master, of an impulse, which I detested, yet could not disobey."

(Chap 25, par 63)

"But now that virtue has become to me a shadow and that happiness and affection are turned into bitter and loathing despair, in what should I seek for sympathy? I am content to suffer alone while my sufferings shall endure: when I die, I am well satisfied that abhorrence and opprobrium should load my memory. Once my fancy was soothed with dreams of virtue, of fame, and of enjoyment. Once I falsely hoped to meet with beings who, pardoning my outward form, would love me for the excellent qualities which I was capable of unfolding. I was nourished with high thought of honor and devotion. But now crime has degraded me beneath the meanest animal. No guilt, no mischief, no malignity, no misery, can be found comparable to mine."

(Chap 24, par 65)

What a magnificent exposition of the logic of the shadow! The BTK serial killer wrote to police decades before his arrest, *"I can't stop it so the monster goes on and hurts me as well as society."* (*The Washington Post,* 27 February 2005.) The shadow has an inexorable need to live, whether in virtue or vice.

Each man has a choice: To remain unconscious of his inner monster and suffer the consequences, or to integrate the forces of his inner monster and find an acceptable outlet for such energy. The monster continues his address to Victor's corpse:

"You hate me; but your abhorrence cannot equal that with which I regard myself. I look on the hands which executed the deed; I think on the heart in which the imagination of was conceived, and long for the moment when these hands

will meet my eyes, when that imagination will haunt my
thoughts no more."

(Chap 24, par 67)

In classical tragedy, the denouement requires the arrival of a
character to constellate a new order. In *Hamlet* Fortinbras arrives
to save Denmark. In *Frankenstein* the novel concludes with Walton
changing the course to return his ship to safety. The monster departs
Walton's ship. Now that his retribution is complete in Victor's death,
the monster plans to build a funeral pyre and die in flames.

> "Some years ago, when the images which this world affords
> first opened upon me, when I felt the cheering warmth
> of summer, and heard the rustling of the leaves and the
> warbling of the birds, and these were all to me, I should
> have wept to die; now it is my only consolation. Polluted
> by crimes, and torn by the bitterest remorse, where can I
> find rest but in death?"

(Chap 24, par 68)

Heaven is on earth; it is the experience of joy. Hell also is of
earth; it is despair. In the Coppula's 1991 *Frankenstein* film the final
scene shows the monster and Victor's corpse burning together on an
iceberg.

NOTES FOR CHAPTER 24

1. There is an inexorable and life-long relationship between the
monster and the ego.

Question: Have you befriended your monster?

2. A man who fails to adequately integrate his shadow will eventually
feel cold and rigid as if on an ice floe; his feeling function is dead.

Question: Have you accepted that your aliveness/animation necessarily
includes finding outlets for your shadow libido?

ictor was a young man with the potential for a joyous life. He could have been assisted through therapy to have grieved his mother's death and come to a peaceful acceptance of his own mortality and to see his own life as separate from his parents. He might have learned he had a personal obligation to serve his Self over what his mother would have him do.

Therapy could have helped Victor understand how his mother had invaded his boundaries with her plans that he should marry Elizabeth, and advised Victor that he is too young and immature at eighteen to commit to marriage. He might best await such thoughts until they arise naturally from his soul.

A competent therapist would have encouraged Victor to pursue his heart's desire for education, especially his affection for the alchemy, thus supporting his psyche's longing for inner reflection. Victor's anxiety over disappointing his father could have lessened by a therapist's empathy to bring Victor the self-permission to follow his own path. His depth psychologist could have instructed him on his inferior function and transformed his adoration of Henry to a fondness for his inner Henry.

When Victor's science prowess led him towards creating the monster, his therapist could have insisted that Victor recognize the personal and moral aspects of his creation, suggesting he consult professors beyond Krempe and Waldman to assess unforeseen problems of creating a monster, and insist he place the good of civilization before personal pride.

Effective therapy could have taught Victor about the intra-psychic nature of his shadow and warn him that its integration might consume years of therapy, likely requiring the techniques dream interpretation, active imagination, and mandala constructions. When Victor's monster requested a female companion, anima integration could have produced a positive outcome. And when the events in Victor's life involved boredom, re-discovering his inner child might have allowed him a renewed appreciation and awe of nature.

Aeschylus's play, *Prometheus Unbound* provides a sequel to the myth of Prometheus. It begins with Prometheus's predicament of chained to a rock with eagles pecking out his liver each day to an ending where Hercules kills Zeus' eagle and frees Prometheus. The moral of the play is that although gaining the knowledge of fire created many problems, eventually the world was made better. Modern therapy is like Hercules: it has the power to remove the pecking insults from the angry god of an unlived unconscious. The outcome is a better world for the individual and for the collective.

Re-Membering Frankenstein is my contribution to those undergoing the Herculean task of therapy. Books cannot replace the value of a competent therapist and the necessary hours along the winding road of Self discovery. Having read this book, I hope you have a greater ability to complete the labors.

There is always hope clinging to the bottom of Pandora's box.

WORKS CITED

Bly, Robert, *IRON JOHN*. First Vintage Books, 1990.

Bolen, Jean Shinida, *GODDESSES IN EVERYWOMAN*. Harper-Row, 1984.

Edinger, Edward, *THE CHRISTIAN ARCHETYPE*. Inner City Books, 1987.

Hendrix, Harville, *GETTING THE LOVE YOU WANT*. Owl Books, 2001.

Hollis, James, *WHY GOOD PEOPLE DO EVIL*, Putman Books, 2007.

Johnson, Robert, *INNER WORK*. Harper-Row, 1986.

JOY. Harper-Row, 1993.

Sheehy, Gail, *NEW PASSAGES*. Thorndike Press, 1977.

UNDERSTANDING MEN'S PASSAGES, ThorndikePress,1998.

Shelley, Mary Wollstonecraft, *FRANKENSTEIN, the NEW PROMETHEUS*

Wolf, Leonard, *THE ESSENTIAL FRANKENSTEIN*. IBooks, Inc. 1977.

Active imagination, 7, trench coat man 89, anima not wife 100, divine child 118,
    saboteur 126, with vampire 156
Anima, exercises 228-229, 239, 244-245
Archetypes, definitions, 7
Arrogance, ego protection, 24

Bly, Robert, author 35, 168
Byron, Lord, 8, 9

Campbell, Joseph, author, bliss 104
Curses, 135
Complexes, definition 7

Divine child, 7, 108-117, exercises 129
Dragon metaphor, 72, 78
Dreams, complex ski track puzzle 16, arrogant driver to bat cave 20, skier
    at bottom of hill 25, sub-rosa rage at Nazis 25, half-finished lakeside
    house 30, mother in the dunking booth 48, surgeon's mother-complex
    46, French girl anima figure 55, prisoners in the basement 64, trench
    coat man 86, Frankenstein95, Victor's of Elizabeth and his mother's
    corpse 97, murder of Nancy Sinatra 100, anima not wife 100, lost child
    116-118, vampire 125, Canadian aliens 125, mountain top space aliens
    126, saboteur 126, multi-generational 131, father as derelict 137, abusive
    accident by police/father 142, burning factory 144, woman drowning in
    waves 145, women with severed hands 146, mountain people 154, boy in

pipe 163, murder and cover-up 169, man raped by football player 172, eye cancer patients 183, moving covered wagons over a lake 200, sun porch 201, skiing on iced concrete 201, puppy 202, little girl movie 210, phone voice 217, mummy movie 220, three women at a café 221, two mirrors 223, gay twin 224, bees in ceiling 226

Edinger, Edward, author, inferior function and joy 106, Christian archetype 160
Ego, definition 6
Elizabeth, 58
Eros, 29, 202

Father-complex, 69, 104, 132-136, exercises 139-140, exercises 213
Feminine justice, 142-147

Grail myth, 106

Hamlet, cursed 97, father-complex 104, 135, 159, 236
Hendrix, Harville, author, 238
Henry Clerval, metaphor 103

Icarus, 22, 78
Ice Queen, 221
Inferior function, exercises 233

Janus, as persona 96
Jerry McGuire, 212
Johnson, Robert, author, 92, 146, 217
Jung, C.G., archetypes 8, apotropaism 220, 221, 253
Justine, 141-144

Kairos, 236
Krempe, professor, 74,111
Kronus, 209

Lunacy, 219

Male friendship, 28
Mandala, 202, exercise 205
Medusa, 221
Moore, Robert, author, 93, 224
Mother, dark 68, 219-220
Mother-complex, 46-59, notes 60
Murder-suicide, 242

Pandora, 12
Panic, 208
Paranoia, 219
Parental Complexes, 69-70, 108
Patriarchy, 185, 220
Polodori, John, 8,9
Pueraeternis, 116
Pullman, Phillip, author, 38
Prometheus, Unbound, 10, myth11
Psyche, definition, 6

Rapture, 80
Relapse tendency, 112

Sea captain story, 35
Shadow, definition 6, exercises 174
Sheehy, Gail, author, 34
Shelley, Mary, author history 7
Shelley, Percy Bysshe, 8
Spirit, definition 7
Soul, definition 6
Synchronicity, Henry 103

Trench Coat Man, 88

Walton, Robert, 15
Waldeman, professor 75-76
Werewolf, 221